Academic Applications

WITH

Technology

JOHN
STEFFEE
ROBERT E. LEE
HIGH SCHOOL
TYLER, TEXAS

SOUTH-WESTERN
EDUCATIONAL PUBLISHING

ISBN: 0-538-64716-7

1 2 3 4 5 6 7 8 9 10 BN 00 99 98 97 96 95

Printed in the United States of America

Managing Editor: Janie F. Schwark
Developmental Editor: Angela McDonald
Production Editor: Becky E. Peveler
Marketing Manager: Brad Van Alfen
Internal Design: Ann Small
Production Artist: Sophia Renieris
Consulting Editor: Bob Sandman
Production Services: Electro-Publishing
Cover Design: Tin Box Studio

I(T)P
International Thomson Publishing

South-Western Educational Publishing is a division of International Thomson Publishing, Inc. The ITP trademark is used under license.

Introduction

You learn best by doing. You probably didn't learn to ride a bicycle by reading about it or memorizing instructions on how to ride it. You learned to ride a bicycle by riding a bicycle. When did you get good at using a calculator? Was it when you read the instruction manual or when you used a calculator to solve problems? You learn to use computer software in the same way.

PURPOSE OF BOOK

Academic Applications with Technology helps you learn to use computer software as a problem-solving tool. The activities in this book provide you with the opportunity to build your computer skills as you build your communications, mathematics, problem-solving, and interpersonal skills. As you work through the activities, you are required to interact well with team members. In many activities, your success and the success of others depend on everyone doing their part. To be successful in society and in the work place, good teamwork skills are essential.

The materials presented in *Academic Applications with Technology* help you understand that the subjects you study at school are not isolated in a particular classroom. It is important that you practice and apply language arts, social studies, and mathematics skills in a variety of situations.

The materials also prepare you for the type of computer situations you will encounter outside the classroom. Today's workers often utilize several different types of software to complete a job. In some activities in this book, you may need to use more than one application software. You will learn to select the best type of software for accomplishing a task. The three software tools with which you will be working will be word processing, database, and spreadsheet.

WORD PROCESSING

Word processing is used primarily to prepare documents. It is one of the most widely used of all computer applications because it makes the writing and revising of documents faster and easier than using a typewriter or pen and paper. You can use the editing features of the word processor to change, add, move, copy, or delete anything you have written.

You will use the word processor to improve your communication and written comprehension skills. When you use the editing features of the word processor, you will be able to improve and to make corrections to your documents. As you use tabs, you will learn to present information in an effective manner. You will use the word processor to develop descriptive, persuasive, and comparative compositions. By using the activities, you will find your language arts skills improving as you improve your computer skills.

DATABASE

A database is like an electronic filing cabinet. It is an organized collection of related facts. Databases are used to enable us to locate information more quickly than we would be able to do manually. A database locates information, organizes data, prints reports, and can, by performing calculations, create new data.

You will use database software to store and organize data on countries, houses, and people. You will create one database on units of measurement which you can use as a reference for completing other activities. You will add records to a database, delete records from a database, sort a database, and create reports. You will use the database to help you locate and present information.

SPREADSHEET

Spreadsheet software allows you to perform mathematical operations quickly and accurately. You can enter text and numbers. By entering formulas you can have the computer rapidly perform mathematical operations. Spreadsheet software also has built-in functions in which complex formulas are already written and available for your use.

Although the spreadsheet is very powerful, it is important that the data and formulas are entered correctly. The activities in this book build your skills as you use spreadsheet software to solve problems. You will learn to enter formulas to produce the right answer. You will also learn to format the answers and represent data graphically. You will find your mathematics skills improving along with your computer skills.

INTERPERSONAL SKILLS

You will also have a chance to improve your interpersonal skills. Employers are asking for people who can work as part of a team. Just as a sports team cannot expect to be successful without practice, you cannot expect to learn to work with others without practice. You will be involved in activities in which everyone must work together and share responsibility in order to succeed. You will need to learn to make suggestions for improvement and learn to accept criticism.

OVERVIEW OF BOOK

This book is divided into three units. The following is a brief description of each unit.

Unit I

You will practice introductory word processing, database, and spreadsheet skills. The word processing activities are designed to improve language arts skills. You will also work with other students in a team to write a descriptive composition. In this unit, you will set up databases that will be used in later activities. In one database activity, you use your problem-solving skills to determine the data to enter. The spreadsheet activities will build your math skills. You will learn how to use spreadsheet software to make quick calculations in problems involving proportions, measurements, statistics, fractions, and geometric figures. In the concluding spreadsheet activity, you will participate with other students in an adventure game in which you track down a gang of computer hackers.

Unit II

You will practice changing the appearance of text in a document. You will boldface and underline text. You will also practice using the find and replace feature of the word processor. In one activity you will use find and replace to decode a document. In another activity you and other students will learn to write an effective persuasive composition. The database activities provide opportunities to make revisions to the databases you created in Unit I. You will learn to use spreadsheet software to make calculations required to become a wise consumer. The spreadsheet activities help you see the true cost of making major purchases such as a home and a car.

Unit III

The word processing activities involve formatting text in a document. You will practice setting and using tabs and various types of indents. The writing composition is a comparative paper. You will practice presenting data graphically by using spreadsheet software. You will create pie, bar, and line charts. The database software will be used to create reports. There is a series of activities in which you will use your database, spreadsheet, and word processing skills to build your geography skills. At the conclusion of this unit is a business simulation. You will work with other students to operate a business selling computers. You will use spreadsheet software to help you make wise business decisions, maintain your records, and produce reports.

SUMMARY

We live in the information age. This means you must be able to locate and use information. You may need to start viewing the role of your teacher differently. Your teacher is not there to dispense information but to provide you the opportunity to learn. Learning is a not restricted to high school, college, or trade school. Learning is a life-long process. You must take the responsibility for your own learning. Your success in life depends on it.

REQUIREMENTS FOR USING THIS BOOK

Academic Applications with Technology is a generic set of exercises covering word processing, database, and spreadsheet skills. It is designed to provide you with practice using commands and features of these applications that you have learned during a class lecture or from a tutorial book. An optional template disk is available from South-Western Educational Publishing. A template disk for either the IBM or Macintosh environment may be ordered. It contains directories for the following programs:

IBM

Microsoft Works Versions 2.0 and 3.0 for Windows
WordPerfect Works Version 2.0 for Windows
ClarisWorks for Windows
Lotus 1-2-3 for Windows, Release 4
Microsoft Works DOS Version 2.0
dBASE IV DOS Version 2.0

Macintosh

Microsoft Works Version 3.0
ClarisWorks Version 2.0

You may be using either a PC-based system or a Macintosh system. Your system may be a stand-alone or may be linked to a network. If you are using a networked computer, your teacher will give you special instructions about how the network works and how *Academic Applications with Technology* should be used with that system.

You should have a formatted disk on which to save your work. If you are saving the exercises on a hard disk (either in your computer or as part of a network), you will receive specific instructions from your teacher.

USING THIS BOOK WITH OR WITHOUT THE TEMPLATE DISK

Academic Applications with Technology may be used with or without the template disk. The template disk does not include a file for every exercise in the book. For exercises where a template file exists, instructions are given how to open the template file. All exercises can be completed whether or not the template disk is used.

All files on the template disk are stored in directories or folders. For the IBM template disk, the files are located by changing to the correct directory. The following directories are used

For Works 2.0 Windows	WORKWIN2
For Works 3.0 Windows	WORKWIN3
For WordPerfect Works	WPWORKS
For ClarisWorks	CLARIS
For Lotus 1-2-3	LOTUS
For Works 2.0 DOS	WORKDOS2
For dBASE IV	DBASE

For the Macintosh template disk, the files are located by changing to the correct folder. The following folders are used

For Microsoft Works	MSWORKS
For ClarisWorks	CLARIS

CREATING A DIRECTORY (IBM) OR FOLDER (MACINTOSH)

You will need to prepare your own data disk on which you will save the exercises that you enter or modify. All exercises will be saved to a directory or folder. If instructed by your teacher, you should add a **DATA** directory or folder to the data disk you receive. If you do not receive a data disk, create a DATA Directory or folder on a blank, formatted disk.

- For DOS computers: Make sure that the DOS prompt shows the letter or the drive where your data disk is located. Key **md DATA** at the DOS prompt to make a directory. Type **cd DATA** at the DOS prompt to change to the DATA directory.

- For Macintosh computers: Make sure the floppy disk or folder where you will store your data is active. Choose New Folder from the File menu. Key **DATA**.

- For Windows computers: In File Manager, select the drive icon for the drive where your data disk is located. From the File Menu, choose Create Directory. When the Create Directory dialog box appears, enter **DATA** and choose the OK button.

- For basic software information, see Appendix A, B, and C.

Contents

Unit 2

Unit 3

Unit 3, continued

Unit

OneTwoThree

123

Activity 3-46

CONCLUSIONS

As a team, write a paper on how your company did. Use a spreadsheet to calculate the total number of each model of computer you sold. Produce a pie chart showing the number of each model of computer sold. Incorporate the pie chart into your word processing document. Incorporate into your document a line graph showing your gross profit for the four weeks. Tell what you would do differently. Do you think your company was successful? On what criteria do you base your success? Give reasons for your success or lack of success.

Save your document as **CK3-46** and print your document.

Objectives

In this section, you will practice the following word processing skills:

- Open new and existing word processing documents
- Enter, typeover, insert, delete, italic, cut, and paste
- Print and save documents

In this section, you will build the following academic skills:

- Recognize appropriate spelling, capitalization, punctuation, and sentence construction within the context of a written passage
- Read for understanding
- Generate a written descriptive composition
- Use a calculator
- Demonstrate an understanding of measurement concepts using metric and customary units

Activity 1-1

Start your word processing software and open the file **T101**. If you are not using the template disk, open a new word processing document.

Enter the following document about the computer service technician. Enter the text as shown even though there are mistakes. Do not correct errors. Your margins may be different from the document. Do not press the Enter key until you reach the end of the paragraph.

```
   The computer service technician maintains and repair
the equipment in a system. Any complex equipment requires
regular maintenance to keep it running properly.
Breakdowns are sure to happen from time to time anyway.
The service technician must troubleshoot, determined the
problem, analyze, and replaces damaged parts. This all
must be done quickly so that the office or business can
continue its work. When an office was part of a network,
with its computers linked to many others, speedy repairs
and minimum down-time is even more critical.
```

Activity 3-45

WEEK 4—KEEPING TRACK OF BUSINESS

Complete the following steps:

1. Copy Form 2 and place it below the data for week three. This will be used for week four. Be sure to label the new spreadsheet data as Week 4.

2. Obtain the information for the sales calculation spreadsheet, and enter the number of units of each computer sold in Form 2 for week four.

3. Calculate the amount of income you earned and your gross profit. Save the spreadsheet as **Form2-4**.

4. Produce a line graph showing your gross profit for the four weeks. Save your work as **CK3-45**.

5. Copy the inventory spreadsheet (Form 4) and place it below week three. The Beginning Inventory for week four will be the same as the Ending Inventory for week three. Enter the Number Assembled and Number Sold and calculate the Ending Inventory. Save the spreadsheet as **Form4-4**.

6. Copy the cash available spreadsheet (Form 5) and place it below week three. The Beginning Cash for week four will be the same as the Cash Balance of week three. Calculate the Cash Balance for week four. Save the spreadsheet as **Form5-4**.

Proofread the document when it is completed. Use the typeover and delete functions of the word processor to correct faulty shifts in verb tense or incorrect subject-verb agreement.

Save the document as **WP1-01**. Close the file.

Activity 3-44

WEEK 4—MAKING BUSINESS DECISIONS

Complete the following steps:

1. Forecast sales for week four.
2. Determine the number of units you have available for sale.
3. Decide what you need to order for the next week.
4. Copy the order form and place it below week three.
5. Complete the order form and print the form. Make sure your order does not exceed your available cash. Save the spreadsheet as **Form1-4**.
6. Discuss with your team the retail price you should charge for each unit.
7. Complete and print the sales entry spreadsheet (Form 3).
8. Enter the information from the sales entry spreadsheet into the sales calculation spreadsheet.

Activity 1-2

Open the document about the service technician, **WP1-01**, and add the following paragraphs a double space below the last paragraph. Enter the paragraphs exactly as shown. Your margins may vary.

```
    Technicians often help set up the systems They must
hook up and test the new equipment. They must be able to
read and understand technical manuels. The must know how
to use specialized tools. Manufactures are constandly
upgrading their machines and methods and the service
technicians must keep up with these improvements.

    The ability to think logically is essential to a good
computer service technician. The technician may be
trained at a technical school on-the-job or by computer
manufacturers courses. Skiled technicians are a vital
part of the computer industry  Many people who start
their carreers as technicians work up to desining systems
or doing other sophisticated jobs in the industry.
```

After you have entered the paragraphs, correct any errors in punctuation and spelling. If you have access to a spell checker or Grammatik, use these features of the software.

You will need to click on Save as to save the document as **WP1-02**. Close the file.

Activity 3-43

WEEK 3—KEEPING TRACK OF BUSINESS

Complete the following steps:

1. Copy Form 2 and place it below the data for week two. This will be used for week three. Be sure to label the new spreadsheet data as Week 3.

2. Obtain the information from the sales calculation spreadsheet, and enter the number of units of each computer sold in Form 2 for week three.

3. Calculate the amount of income you earned, and your gross profit. Save the spreadsheet as **Form2-3**.

4. Produce a bar graph showing the income in dollars for the first three weeks. Print another bar graph showing your gross profit for the first three weeks. Save your work as **CK3-43**.

5. Copy the inventory spreadsheet (Form 4) and place it below week two. The Beginning Inventory for week three will be the same as the Ending Number for week two. Enter the Number Assembled and Number Sold, and calculate the Ending Inventory. Save the spreadsheet as **Form4-3**.

6. Copy the cash available spreadsheet (Form 5) and place it below week two. The Beginning Cash for week three will be the same as the Cash Balance of week two. Calculate the Cash Balance for week three. Save the spreadsheet as **Form5-3**.

Activity 1-3

Open the document **WP1-02**. Enter the following questions a double-space below the last paragraph. Enter the number of the question, a period, and two spaces. Do not skip lines between the questions.

1. Which is the best meaning of *critical* in the first paragraph?
2. Which is the best definition of *logically* in paragraph three?
3. The author probably wrote this article to ____.
4. Which of these is true about this selection?
5. Which is an opinion presented in the article?

From the answers for each question listed below, select the correct answer. Insert a blank line between the answer and the next question. Then begin keying the correct answer on the line under the question. Remember not to skip a line between questions. Save the completed document as **WP1-03**. Close the file.

Question 1

a. finding fault with
b. dangerously ill
c. telling about movies or books
d. very important

Question 2

a. using mathematics
b. in a reasonable, orderly way
c. argumentative
d. having great intelligence

Question 3

a. Tell about famous computer technicians
b. Persuade people to choose a career in computers
c. Give information about a career field
d. Complain about problems computer technicians face in their jobs

Question 4

a. The setting is a large office in the year 1990.
b. Computer manuals have funny cartoons in them.
c. The main character in this story is Ted the Technician.
d. This is a factual article about a career field.

Question 5

a. The computer industry thinks highly of skilled technicians.
b. Computer technicians do not need a college degree.
c. A person who doesn't want to move up in his career field is not working hard.
d. A computer repair person has to be smarter than an automobile mechanic.

Activity 3-42

WEEK 3—MAKING BUSINESS DECISIONS

Complete the following steps:

1. Forecast sales for week three.
2. Determine the number of units you have available for sale.
3. Decide what you need to order for the next week.
4. Copy the order form and place it below week two.
5. Complete the order form and print the form. Make sure your order does not exceed your available cash. Save the spreadsheet as **Form1-3**.
6. Discuss with your team the retail price you should charge for each unit.
7. Complete and print the sales entry spreadsheet (Form 3).
8. Enter the information from the sales entry spreadsheet into the sales calculation spreadsheet.

Activity 1-4

Start your word processing software and open the template file **T104**. If you are not using the template disk, open a new word processing document and enter the following two paragraphs about the systems analyst.

```
   A systems analyst is a coordinator which helps people
and machines work together to solve problems and process
data. Systems analysts design programs to fit particular
needs. They look at what a company, or user, wants its
computers to do. They talk to the people which will be
operating the system, and they look at the equipment
which is available.

   The analyst will plan the database and determine what
kind of information is to go into the system, what is to
come out of them and the analyst may work with
programmers. Telling those how to write programs for the
system. The systems analyst may suggest guidelines for
the operators to follow.
```

Correct any run-on sentences or sentence fragments. Change any incorrect case of pronouns.

Print the document. Save the document as **WP1-04**. Close the file.

5. Copy the inventory spreadsheet (Form 4) and place it below week one. The Beginning Inventory for week two will be the same as the Ending Number for week one. Enter the Number Assembled and the Number Sold, and calculate the Ending Inventory. Look at the following example. Save the spreadsheet as **Form4-2**.

Form 4

	A	B	C	D	E
1	Week 1	Begin	Number	Number	Ending
2		Inventory	Assembled	Sold	Inventory
3	Model				
4	Model 1	0	10	6	4
5	Model 2	0	3	2	1
6	Model 3	0	3	2	1
7	Model 4	0	2	1	1
8	Model 5	0	2	1	1
9					
10					
11	Week 2	Begin	Number	Number	Ending
12		Inventory	Assembled	Sold	Inventory
13	Model				
14	Model 1	4			
15	Model 2	1			
16	Model 3	1			
17	Model 4	1			
18	Model 5	1			

6. Copy the cash available spreadsheet (Form 5) and place it below week one. The Beginning Cash for week two will be the same as the Cash Balance of week one. Calculate the Cash Balance for week two. Save the spreadsheet as **Form5-2**.

Activity 1-5

Open the document **WP1-04**.

Add the following two paragraphs to the document.

```
   An analyst can have a degree technical school degree
computer manufacturers training, or on-the-job training
This person may have skills or training in business
engineering mathematics science or computer science The
analyst may work for a computer company helping customers
get their systems set up and working or may be employed
by a large company overseeing its computer activities.

   A career as systems analyst is a profitable job for
one who has skills in using computers and who is willing
to get additional training to learn more There are
several ways to get training and there are many jobs in
industry for a good systems analyst.
```

Correct any punctuation errors.

From the choices listed below, select the best main idea for this article and key it a double-space below the text.

a. A systems analyst is trained to help people and machines work together to solve problems and process data.

b. A systems analyst can have on-the-job training.

c. A systems analyst may work for a computer company or for a large company that uses many computers.

d. The analyst plans the database.

Activity 3-41

WEEK 2—KEEPING TRACK OF BUSINESS

Complete the following steps:

1. Copy Form 2 and place it below the data for week one. This will be used for week two. Be sure to label the spreadsheet as Week 2. Look at the following example. Your numbers will vary.

	A	B	C	D	E	F	G
1	Week 1		Retail	Unit	Number		Gross
2	Model	Cost	Price	Profit	Sold	Income	Profit
3	Model 1	982	1,082	100.00	6	6,492	600
4	Model 2	1,097	1,199	102.00	2	2,398	204
5	Model 3	1,102	1,295	193.00	2	2,590	386
6	Model 4	1,412	1,599	187.00	1	1,599	187
7	Model 5	1,467	1,649	182.00	1	1,649	182
8					Totals	14,728	1,559
9							
10	Week 2		Retail	Unit	Number		Gross
11	Model	Cost	Price	Profit	Sold	Income	Profit
12	Model 1						
13	Model 2						
14	Model 3						
15	Model 4						
16	Model 5						
17					Totals		

2. Obtain the information from the sales calculation spreadsheet, and enter the number of units of each computer sold in Form 2 for week two.

3. Calculate the amount of income you earned and your gross profit. Save the spreadsheet as **Form2-2**.

4. Produce a line graph showing your amount of income in dollars (total amount of money you made) and your profit for week one and week two. Save your work as **CK3-41**.

From the choices listed below, select a detail from the article and key it a double-space below the main idea.

a. The systems analyst repairs computers.

b. The systems analyst must have excellent keyboarding skills.

c. The systems analyst deals with machines but not with people.

d. The systems analyst tells programmers how to write the needed programs.

Print the document. Save the document as **WP1-05**. Close the file.

Discuss with your team the retail price you should charge for each unit. Complete the sales entry spreadsheet (Form 3). The number of units available for sale will be determined by adding the number of each model not sold the first week to the number of units you assemble from the component parts you have purchased. Enter the information in the sales calculation spreadsheet.

Activity 1-6

Start your word processing software and open the template file **T106**. If you are not using the template disk, open a new document and enter the letter exactly as shown below. The date line should be keyed at the top of your monitor. The margins may not be the same as the word processor you are using, so the lengths of the lines may vary slightly.

```
October 19, 19—

Jim Dandy Auto Parts Store
1412 Thirteenth Street
Houston, Texas 77777-0910

Ladies and Gentlemen:

We are unabel to fill you're order for 6,000 carburetors
and 1,400 rubber gascets at this time. These items are
beeing placed on backorder with our companie and will be
shipped as soon as the items are available.

The rest of your order is compleat, however, and will
leeve our store by UPS today. You should receave your
parts within a few days. Thank you for your order. We
appreshiate the opertunity to do business with you.

Sincearly,



John D. Biznezman
```

Replace the name at the end of the letter with your name and print the letter.

After the original document has been entered, correct the spelling errors in the document.

Print the corrected document. Save the document as **WP1-06**. Close the file.

Activity 3-40

WEEK 2—MAKING BUSINESS DECISIONS

Forecast sales for the second week. Determine the number of units you have available to sell the second week. Decide what you need to order for the next week. Copy Form 1 to create a new form below the order form for week one. Calculate the cost of the order for week two and print your order. Check your cash available worksheet to make sure the cost of the order does not exceed the amount of money you have.

	A	B	C	D
1		Order		
2	Week 1			
3		Cost	Quantity	Extension
4	Power Supply			
5	Monitor			
6	Mouse			
7	Keyboard			
8	Hard Drive			
9	Mboard 386SX			
10	Mboard 486SX			
11	Mboard 486DX			
12	I/O Card			
13	VGA Card			
14	Floppy 3.5			
15	Floppy 5.25			
16	Memory			
17	Cost of Order			
18				
19		Order		
20	Week 2			
21		Cost	Quantity	Extension
22	Power Supply			
23	Monitor			
24	Mouse			
25	Keyboard			
26	Hard Drive			
27	Mboard 386SX			
28	Mboard 486SX			
29	Mboard 486DX			
30	I/O Card			
31	VGA Card			
32	Floppy 3.5			
33	Floppy 5.25			
34	Memory			
35	Cost of Order			

Activity 1-7

Start your word processing software and open the template file **T107**. If you are not using the template disk, open a new document and enter the following. Enter the numbers needed to complete the equivalent measurements and the conversions. Enter as many of the numbers as you know.

Linear Measure

1 foot = inches
1 yard = feet
1 rod = yards
1 furlong = rods
1 mile = yards = feet = furlongs
1 league = land miles
1 international nautical mile = feet

Liquid Measure

1 tablespoon = teaspoons
1 cup = fluid ounces
1 pint = cups = fluid ounces
1 quart = pints = cups
1 gallon = quarts = pints = fluid ounces

Conversions

1 inch = centimeters
1 kilometer = miles
1 meter = inches = yards
1 mile = kilometers
1 yard = meters
1 cubic inch = cubic centimeters
1 cubic foot = cubic centimeters = cubic meters
1 cubic yard = cubic meters
1 fluid ounce = milliliters = liters
1 pint liquid = liters
1 quart = liters
1 gallon = liters

Save the document as **WP1-07**. Close the file.

The Beginning Cash for the first week will be the amount you borrow from the bank. The Disbursements will include the amount spent to purchase parts, your rent, and your weekly loan payment. These should be totaled. Next to Sales for Week, enter the amount of income from sales for the week. The Cash Balance is the Beginning Cash minus Total Cash Disbursements, plus Sales for Week.

Form 5

	A	B
1	Beginning Cash	
2	Disbursements	
3	Purchases	
4	Rent	
5	Loan Payment	
6	Total Cash Disbursements	
7		
8	Sales for Week	
9		
10	Cash Balance	

Save the cash available spreadsheet as **Form5**.

Activity 1-8

Start your word processing software and open the template file **T108**. If you are not using the template disk, open a new word processing document and enter the following phrases that describe when various types of punctuation should be used. Also enter the names of the punctuation marks.

At the end of a sentence expressing strong feeling
Before a list of words or phrases
After a series of introductory prepositional phrases
After an introductory participial phrase
After an introductory dependent clause
At the end of complete declarative sentences
At the end of direct questions, statements ending with a question, or words or sentences that indicate a question
After an introductory word
To set off the name of a person spoken to
Before a direct quotation
After each number or letter that begins a heading in an outline
Between city and state
Between the day and year in a date
After the closing of a letter
To separate independent clauses not joined by a coordinating conjunction
After initials, abbreviations, and after each part of some abbreviations
After the opening (salutation) of a business letter
After the opening of a friendly letter
To set off nonrestrictive appositives and parenthetical expressions
To set off nonessential clauses and phrases
To separate coordinate adjectives
Between the hour and minutes expressing time

Activity 3-39

WEEK 1—KEEPING TRACK OF BUSINESS

Get a copy of the number of units of each model you sold from your teacher. Use these figures to calculate your total sales in dollars and your total profit. Using spreadsheet Form 2, enter the number of units of each model computer you actually sold. The spreadsheet should calculate your income from sales and the gross profit. Be sure to label the spreadsheet as Week 1. Save the file as **Form2-1**.

Create and print a pie chart showing the quantities of each model sold. Make sure the name of your company is on the chart. Save the chart as **CK3-39**.

Create an inventory spreadsheet. The spreadsheet should list each model, the beginning inventory, the number assembled, the number sold, and ending inventory. The beginning inventory are the computers you had on hand that did not sell the previous week. The beginning inventory for the first week is zero for each model. The ending inventory is calculated by adding the beginning inventory to the number of computers you assembled, and subtracting the number sold. Save the inventory spreadsheet as **Form4-1**.

Form 4

	A	B	C	D	E
1	Company Name	Begin	Number	Number	Ending
2		Inventory	Assembled	Sold	Inventory
3	Model				
4	Model 1				
5	Model 2				
6	Model 3				
7	Model 4				
8	Model 5				

Create a cash available spreadsheet. The purpose of this spreadsheet will be to maintain an accurate record of cash. You will need to know how much cash you have available to purchase inventory and operate your business. This will also show how much cash you will have to live on.

Between independent clauses joined by a coordinating conjunction

In a series of words, phrases, or clauses

Period

Question Mark

Exclamation Point

Colon

Semicolon

Comma

Use cut and paste to place the phrases below the appropriate type of punctuation.

Save the file as **WP1-08**. Close the file.

Activity 3-38

WEEK 1—SALES ENTRY FORM

Discuss as a team the prices for each model. You do not need to have the same amount of profit on each model. You will be able to change your prices from week to week or have a "special" on a different model each week. After you have determined the amount for which you are going to sell each unit of each model, put that amount and the number of units of each model you have available to sell on a new spreadsheet. The first week, the units available for sale (Units on Hand) will be the number of units of each model you have assembled. This spreadsheet will be the Sales Entry Form. You may use Form 3 as an example.

Form 3

	A	B	C
1	Company Name	Retail	Units on
2	Model	Price	Hand
3	Model 1		
4	Model 2		
5	Model 3		
6	Model 4		
7	Model 5		

Be sure the name of your company is included on the form. When you have completed the form, save the form as **Form3** and print it. Take the Sales Entry Form to the computer that has the sales calculation spreadsheet. These numbers will be entered in that spreadsheet. You must enter the prices and quantities you have printed on the sales calculation spreadsheet. They cannot be changed. Be sure that other teams do not see your numbers before they are entered in the sales calculation spreadsheet.

Activity 1-9

Start your word processing software and open the template file **T109**. If you are not using the template disk, open a new word processing document and enter the inventory of an antique store as shown. Save the document as **WP1-09A**.

After the document is saved, use the cut and paste feature to place the items in order from oldest to newest. Format all entries with the date first, a hyphen, and the description. Each description should begin with a capital letter.

Place your name in the upper right corner of the document and print the file. Save the new document as **WP1-09**. Close the file.

```
Bentwood rocking chair, 1920

1875 - Pair of framed flower prints

1933 - spittoon from saloon in Langtry, Texas

lady's wedding dress, 1900

pearl earrings, 1899

1918 - military buttons from World War I

1913 - birthday card, hand-colored and signed by the

artist

1876 - flag from centennial celebration in Washington
```

Form 2

	A	B	C	D	E	F	G
1			Retail	Unit	Number		Gross
2	Model	Cost	Price	Profit	Sold	Income	Profit
3	Model 1						
4	Model 2						
5	Model 3						
6	Model 4						
7	Model 5						
8					Totals		

Activity 1-10

THE DESCRIPTIVE COMPOSITION—PART I

You will be writing a descriptive composition using the word processor. The nice thing about using the word processor is that you don't have to get it perfect the first time. If changes are needed, you can edit the document and make any needed corrections without rekeying the entire paper.

In this activity you will be working as part of a team. Other students will be helping you improve your paper, and you will be checking the papers of others. Working together as a team will make producing a good paper much easier.

This activity will be done in a series of steps. Some of the time you will be working on the word processor. Other times you will be discussing ways to improve papers with other students and then you will move back to the word processor for corrections and improvements.

Step 1

Write a five-sentence paragraph describing one of the following:

A storm you experienced

The school cafeteria

Your favorite place to eat

Using three lines at the top of the document, enter your name, date, and class period. Place this information flush right on the document. Double-space the document and make sure the document has a one-inch margin on both sides. The lines should be unjustified.

Save the document as **WP1-10A**.

Step 2

Follow your teacher's directions concerning your composition. Make any needed corrections to the document.

Print a copy of the corrected document for each member of the team and save the document as **WP1-10B**.

Activity 3-37

BEATING THE COMPETITION

You have calculated the cost of the parts of each computer. Next, you will need to decide the cost at which you wish to sell the computers. The difference between what you pay for the computer and the price you sell the computer for is your profit. The greater the difference, the greater your profit.

There is one problem, however: competition. There are other people doing the same thing you are doing, and they are the competition. The competition will be represented by the other teams in your room. All of the teams will be trying to sell computers.

How will you know how many computers you sell? Each team will enter their prices for each one of the computers on the sales calculation spreadsheet provided by the teacher. The prices will be compared, and the sales for each week will be determined. The lower the price, the greater the sales.

Determine the unit price for which to sell each model. What retail price would you have to put on the units to earn enough to pay your rent and make your weekly payment on your note? Also consider that you will need to make enough money to live on for a month. If you were living on your own and buying a car, how much money would you need to make each week? Although there may be two or three team members, make your calculations as if only one person owned and ran the business.

Create a spreadsheet in which to place the models and the prices for which they will be sold. The spreadsheet will also have your unit cost for each model. The spreadsheet should calculate the profit on each unit of each model. For example, if a model cost you $925 and you sell it for $1,025, your profit will be $100 per unit. One column will be used to enter the number of each model sold. In this activity, enter the number of units of each model you anticipate selling. Also create a column to calculate the amount of income for each model. Income is calculated by multiplying retail price by number sold. The last column should be the gross profit for each model. Gross profit is calculated by multiplying the number sold by the profit for each unit. Total the income column and profit column. You can use Form 2 as an example. Save your work as **Form2**.

Step 3

The teacher will assign each member of the team a particular responsibility. One will be the Power Word Advisor, one the Mechanics Supervisor, and one the Editorial Assistant. Work with members of your team to make improvements to the papers. Each member of the team has certain items about the paper to check. When you are making suggestions for improvements to others, make the suggestions in a positive, helpful way. Never make fun of someone else's work.

Step 4

Make the necessary corrections and improvements to your paper. Enter the names of the other members of your team flush right at the bottom of the paper. Have the other members of the team check your paper on the screen or on a hard copy (printed document). Print the paper and save the document as **WP1-10**.

Form 1

	A	B	C	D
1		Order		
2				
3		Cost	Quantity	Extension
4	Power Supply			
5	Monitor			
6	Mouse			
7	Keyboard			
8	Hard Drive			
9	Mboard 386SX			
10	Mboard 486SX			
11	Mboard 486DX			
12	I/O Card			
13	VGA Card			
14	Floppy 3.5			
15	Floppy 5.25			
16	Memory			
17				
10	Cost of Order			

Your plan is to assemble enough computers to get started. With the money you get from the sale of computers the first week, you can buy the parts you need to assemble the computers to sell for the next week. Using this plan, you will only need to buy enough parts at the beginning for the computers you anticipate selling the first week.

You have the money needed to set up your booth and buy basic supplies, but you will need money to buy the computer parts. The bank has agreed to loan you up to $25,000 at 10.75% interest. Calculate the weekly payment on the loan if you borrowed the money for one year. You should use the following headings on your spreadsheet.

Principal	Weekly Interest	Term	Weekly Payment

Save your payment calculation as **CK3-36**.

POWER WORD ADVISOR—PART I

Papers are more interesting when details are elaborated with powerful images and figurative language. This can be done by using descriptive verbs, adjectives, and adverbs. An adjective is a word that modifies a noun and an adverb is a word that modifies a verb. Using descriptive verbs, adjectives, and adverbs, writers can make their papers more interesting and colorful.

Figurative language can be used to make a paper more interesting. Two examples of figurative language are similes and personification. A simile uses *like* or *as* to make a comparison (for example, "The raging bull was like a runaway freight train."). Personification gives human qualities to nonhuman things (for example, "The moon winked at us through the night clouds.").

As the Power Word Advisor, it will be your job to make suggestions for making your team members' papers more colorful and interesting. Your suggestions should be specific. Don't just tell the author to use more adverbs or adjectives, but make specific suggestions. You should work with the author of the paper to include a simile or personification in the paper. Use the lists provided on pages 17–19 to find more descriptive verbs and power words to use in the paper.

After you have worked with the other members of your team, fill out the Power Word Advisor Evaluation I form on page 20 for each team member.

Activity 3-36

BORROWING MONEY

You know of a business in another city that is like the one you are starting. That business sold the following computers in an average week:

Model 1	30
Model 2	10
Model 3	10
Model 4	6
Model 5	4

The city in which they are selling has a population of 325,000. The city where you are located has a population of 100,000. Determine the number of each model computer you anticipate selling in your city in one week. You should create a spreadsheet similar to the following example.

	Model 1	Model 2	Model 3	Model 4	Model 5
Sales Forecast					

Next, you will need to prepare your order. List the parts you wish to order, the cost of each part, the quantity of each part ordered, and the extension (which is quantity times price). Calculate the total cost of the parts you will need to buy to assemble the computers you anticipate selling the first week. You may use Form 1 as an example. Save the spreadsheet as **Form1**.

Expressive Verbs

meander
pace
hike
roam
vacate
wander
soar
sneak
descend
stagger
intrude
leap
thrash
rove
nudge
grasp
submerge
hurl
whirl
grind
attribute
rotate
swallow
urge
emerge
wager
rumble
commit
condone
leer
forsake
deprive
warp
trudge
pacify
recall
trace
tease
pry
ply
free
thrust
wedge
hoist
heave
lash
litter
warp
creak
refresh
assign
thwart
slash
tear
thrill
reform
crave
escort
analyze
mend
flog
engender
stitch
collide
discard
pretend
mangle
clip
forfeit
strip
jerk
seduce
dread
unlace
behave
discharge
weep
beam
lament
bewail
twinkle
snooze
slumber
counsel
eye
gaze
survey
endure
aspire
feign
pledge
reprove
entreat
doze
assail
slope
appease
affix
lash
cipher
plunder
determine
recline
slide
hurl
secure
banish
rouse
elate
seep
combine
chasten
guess
implore
recite
ponder
utter
warble
coax
jingle
ripple
whet
pardon
regulate
dominate
strangle
rectify
afflict
chuckle
tilt
gossip
endeavor
confuse
join
frolic
roast
pierce
wreak
overrule
cast
blend
launder
direct
perish
flush
glance
smuggle
approach
discern
debate

Activity 3-35

COMPONENT PRICES

Listed below are the prices of the component parts you need to assemble the computers you will be selling. Refer to the product list to determine the components of each computer. Select the appropriate computer software to calculate the cost of the parts of each one of the computers. Your work should be labeled in such a way as to be easy to understand. Save the file as **CK3-35**.

Enter the name of your company and the names of the team members on your work and print.

Case & Power Supply	60.00
Mother Boards	
386 DX	130.00
486 SX	250.00
486 DX	500.00
Memory	
1 MB	30.00
I/O Card	17.00
VGA Card	40.00
Floppy Drive	
5.25	55.00
3.5	55.00
120 MB Hard drive	280.00
Keyboard	35.00
Monitor SVGA	280.00
Mouse	25.00

Power Words

Happy

festive
contented
relaxed
calm
complacent
satisfied
serene
comfortable
peaceful
joyous
ecstatic
enthusiastic
inspired
glad
pleased
cheerful
excited
cheery
lighthearted
buoyant
carefree
surprised
optimistic
spirited
vivacious
brisk
sparkling
merry
generous
hilarious
exhilarated
jolly
playful
elated
jubilant
thrilled

Eager

avid
earnest
intent
zealous
ardent

Sad

sorrowful
unhappy
depressed
melancholy
gloomy
somber
dismal
quiet
worthless
mournful
dreadful
dreary
flat
blah
dull
sullen
moody
sulky
out of sorts
low
discontent
discouraged
disappointed
concerned
sympathetic
ill at ease
choked up
embarrassed
shameful
ashamed
useless
worthless
heavy hearted

Hurt

injured
isolated
offended
distressed
pained
suffering
afflicted
worried

Angry

resentful
irritated
enraged
furious
annoyed
inflamed
provoked
infuriated
offended
sullen
indignant
irate
wrathful
cross
sulky
frustrated
grumpy
boiling
fuming
stubborn
belligerent
confused
awkward
bewildered

Fearless

encouraged
courageous
confident
secure
independent
reassured
bold
brave
daring
heroic
hardy
determined
loyal
proud
impulsive

Products for Sale

Model 1	386 DX 3.5 floppy 2 MB memory
Model 2	386 DX 3.5 floppy 5.25 floppy 4 MB memory
Model 3	486 SX 3.5 floppy 2 MB memory
Model 4	486 DX 3.5 floppy 4 MB memory
Model 5	486 DX 3.5 floppy 5.25 floppy 4 MB memory

All models are equipped with a mouse, SVGA monitor, I/O card, VGA card, power supply, keyboard, and at least a 120 MB hard drive.

Power Words

Doubtful

unbelieving
skeptical
distrustful
suspicious
dubious
uncertain
questioning
evasive
wavering
hesitant
perplexed
indecisive
hopeless
powerless
helpless
pessimistic

Physical

taut
immobilized
paralyzed
tense
stretched
hollow
empty
strong
weak
sweaty
breathless
nauseated
sluggish
weary
repulsed
tired
alive
feisty
restful

Affectionate

close
loving
tender

Miscellaneous

humble
torn
mixed-up
envious
jealous
preoccupied
cruel
distant
bored
hypocritical
phony
two-faced
cooperative

Afraid

frightened
timid
wishy-washy
shaky
apprehensive
terrified
panicky
tragic
hysterical
alarmed
cautious
shocked
horrified
insecure
impatient
nervous
dependent
anxious
pressured
worried
doubtful
suspicious
gutless
hesitant
awed
dismayed
scared
cowardly

You can expect questions from people who do not know much about computers. It would be helpful to have a flyer describing the five models to give to prospective customers. This flyer should also give an explanation of the terms and why the features are important to a customer. Do not put prices on your flyer. The models you will be selling are described on page 151.

This flyer represents your business, so make it as attractive as possible. Choose a company name and place your company name at the top of the flyer. Use borders or any other feature of the word processor to make your flyer look professional.

Save your flyer as **CK3-34.**

Power Word Advisor
Evaluation I

Name: ______________________________________

Writer's Name: ______________________________________

Date: ______________________

Class Period: ________________

Other verbs you could use are:

The best use of adjectives and adverbs in your paper is when you describe:

Adjectives or adverbs that might be used:

A simile or personification that could be used in your paper might be:

The thing I like best about your paper is:

Objectives

In this section, you will practice the following software skills:

- Use desktop publishing features of your word processing software to produce an advertising flyer
- Create spreadsheets
- Enter formulas in spreadsheets
- Create pie, line, and bar charts

In this section, you will build the following academic skills:

- Organize ideas and demonstrate control of the English language in written compositions
- Solve equations
- Make cost and revenue forecasts
- Maintain business records
- Allocate money and materials
- Analyze or interpret graphs or charts

Activity 3-34

GOING INTO THE COMPUTER BUSINESS

By looking at advertisements in magazines and newspapers, you have found that you can buy the component parts to build computers. You can order these parts, assemble them, and then sell the computers. Assume that you have decided to only sell five different models, so you will not need a large selling space. The selling space should be located where there will be a large number of potential customers.

A kiosk is a small building or booth. You might have seen this type of booth in malls, especially around Christmas. Your team has entered into an agreement with Frank's Discount City to lease a small area in the building. The cost of the space is $150 per week.

MECHANICS SUPERVISOR—PART I

As the Mechanics Supervisor, you will need to check your team members' papers for spelling, punctuation, capitalization, and sentence structure. If necessary refer to the "Punctuation Rules" and "Capitalization Rules" on pages 22–24. After the corrections have been made, you will need to complete the Mechanics Supervisor evaluation form for each paper you have checked.

One aspect of the paper you will be checking is sentence structure. Papers should have a variety of sentence structures. You will need to be able to recognize the various types of sentence structures and work with the author of the paper to create a variety of sentences. It is also important that papers written by members of your team do not contain run-on sentences or sentence fragments.

Sentences can be simple, complex, compound, or compound-complex. A simple sentence is made up of one main clause. It has one subject and one predicate and expresses one main thought. For example:

> **The computers in the room were tan.**

A compound sentence contains two or more main clauses that are equally important and closely related in thought. For example:

> **Learning word processing can take some time, but using a word processor can save time.**

A complex sentence has one main clause and one or more subordinate clauses. For example:

> **Although the dot matrix printer was working as fast as it could, it was still not fast enough for Terry.**

A compound-complex sentence is made up of two or more main clauses and one or more subordinate clauses. For example:

> **Although the dot matrix printer was working as fast as it could, it was still not fast enough for Terry who purchased a laser printer the next day.**

Keep in mind that one type of sentence is not necessarily superior to another. The important thing is to have a variety of sentence structures in a document.

Activity 3-30

Sort the countries by population. Place the six smallest countries by population in a spreadsheet. Produce a bar chart showing the population of the countries. Sort the countries by square miles. Place the six largest countries by area in a spreadsheet. Produce a bar chart of the six largest areas. Save the last chart as **DB3-301, DB3-302, DB3-303,** or **DB3-304**.

Activity 3-31

You will need to create a database for a group of countries with which you have not previously worked. You will set up the database using only the tables produced in Activities 3-28, 3-29, and 3-30. Use the tables to set up a database of 12 countries. The fields will be square miles, population, and male and female life expectancies. Save the database as **DB3-311, DB3-312, DB3-313,** or **DB-314** and print it.

Activity 3-32

Place all the databases in one file or copy them all to the same disk. Place the male and female life expectancies, and percent of arable land in a spreadsheet. Leave out the data on the United States. Find the average male and female life expectancies. Find the average percent of arable land. Write a report comparing what you have found to figures for the United States. What are the factors that influence the figures in your report? Save the report as **DB3-32**.

Activity 3-33

Use the draw program to draw a map of the state in which you live. Include on the map the major cities. Find the population and the area of your state. Place the density at the bottom of the map. Save your work as **DB3-33**.

Punctuation Rules

Period

1. At the end of complete declarative sentences
2. After each number or letter that begins a heading in an outline
3. After initials, abbreviations, and after each part of some abbreviations

Question Mark

At the end of direct questions, statements ending with a question, or words or sentences that indicate a question

Exclamation Point

At the end of a sentence expressing a strong feeling

Colon

1. After the opening (salutation) of a business letter
2. Before a list of words or phrases
3. Between the hour and minutes expressing the time

Semicolon

To separate independent clauses not joined by a coordinating conjunction

Activity 3-27

The figures for arable land in Activity 3-26 were given in percentages. You need to convert this information to the actual numbers. First open your database and sort the records in ascending order by percent of arable land. Create a report using the database. Your report should have the name of the country, the square miles, the population, the percent of arable land, the percent of urban population, and number of square miles of arable land. The number of square miles of arable land will need to be calculated. Enter the group number, *Prepared by*, and your name as the title of the report. Save the file as **DB3-271, DB3-272, DB3-273,** or **DB3-274** and print the files.

Activity 3-28

Sort the countries database by population. Place the six largest countries (in population) in a spreadsheet. Produce a bar chart showing the population of the countries. Sort the countries by square miles. Find the six smallest countries. Place this information in a spreadsheet. Convert the square miles to kilometers. Produce a bar chart showing these countries and their sizes in kilometers. Print the charts. Save your last chart as **DB3-281, DB3-282, DB3-283,** or **DB3-284**.

Activity 3-29

Sort the countries database by male life expectancy. Place the six countries with the longest male life expectancies in one spreadsheet and the six countries with the shortest male life expectancies in another spreadsheet. Create a stacked bar chart showing the male and female life expectancies for each country. Print the charts. Save the last chart as **DB3-291, DB3-292, DB3-293,** or **DB3-294**.

Comma

1. In a series of words, phrases, or clauses
2. Between independent clauses joined by a coordinating conjunction
3. To separate coordinate adjectives (e.g., a cold, rainy day)
4. To set off nonessential clauses and phrases
5. To set off nonrestrictive appositives and parenthetical expressions
6. After the opening of a friendly letter
7. After the closing of a letter
8. Between the day and year in a date
9. Between the city and state
10. Before a direct quotation
11. To set off a name in direct address
12. After an introductory word
13. After a series of introductory prepositional phrases
14. After an introductory participial phrase
15. After an introductory dependent clause

Group 4

Country	Arable land	Urban population
Argentina	.09	.87
Nicaragua	.10	.60
Panama	.06	.53
Paraguay	.20	.46
Venezuela	.04	.83
Brazil	.08	.76
United States	.21	.76
Jamaica	.19	.52
Haiti	.20	.29
Cuba	.29	.72
Honduras	.16	.40
Colombia	.05	.65

Save the database as **DB3-264** and print it.

Capitalization Rules

1. Capitalize proper nouns (e.g., Dallas, Texas).
2. Capitalize proper adjectives (e.g., Mexican food).
3. Capitalize the pronoun *I.*
4. Capitalize words that show family relationships when they are used instead of a name or as part of a name (e.g., I asked Mother if Aunt Mary was coming for Christmas.).

   Do not capitalize words when they are preceded by a possessive, such as *my, your,* or *their* (e.g., My father and cousin were with your aunt.).
5. Capitalize special titles when they immediately precede a name (e.g., General George S. Patton, Congressman Clancy).
6. Capitalize professional titles and their abbreviations when they follow a personal name (e.g., Thomas Crow, R.N., Mary Hopkins, M.D.).
7. Capitalize brand names (e.g., Tandy, Commodore, Lotus).
8. Capitalize the names of all nationalities and races (e.g., Japanese).
9. Capitalize the days of the week, months of the year, and holidays. Use lowercase on seasons of the year (e.g., Memorial Day, spring, fall).
10. Capitalize the first word of a direct quotation (e.g., The teacher said, "First you have to turn on the computer.").
11. Capitalize the first word following a colon if the conventions for capitalizing apply to it (e.g., I discovered what was wrong: The computer did not have enough memory.).
12. Capitalize the first word in the salutation and the first word of the complimentary close of a letter (e.g., Dear Mr. Gutierrez, Sincerely yours).
13. Capitalize the first word and all important words in the titles of works of art, books, magazines, newspapers, poems, songs, articles, television shows, plays, computer software, reports, and other writing (e.g., The Last Supper, "Family Ties," Lotus 1-2-3).

Group 2

Country	Arable land	Urban population
Uganda	.23	.11
Gambia	.16	.21
Algeria	.03	.51
Zimbabwe	.07	.25
Ghana	.05	.33
Liberia	.01	.46
South Africa	.12	.60
Mozambique	.04	.31
Zaire	.03	.44
Egypt	.04	.44
Ethiopia	.13	.11
Chad	.02	.32

Save the database as **DB3-262** and print it.

Group 3

Country	Arable land	Urban population
Cambodia	.16	.20
Indonesia	.08	.31
Iran	.09	.57
India	.57	.28
Vietnam	.23	.20
Philippines	.26	.43
North Korea	.19	.60
Laos	.04	.19
Myanmar	.15	.25
Bangladesh	.67	.24
South Korea	.22	.74
Singapore	.11	.92

Save the database as **DB3-263** and print it.

Mechanics Supervisor
Evaluation I

Name: ______________________________

Writer's Name: ______________________________

Date: ____________________

Class Period: ______________

Spelling that needs correction:

Punctuation that needs correction:

Capitalization that needs correction:

A way you might combine or reword sentences to have greater variety or clarity would be:

A sentence fragment or run-on sentence that needs correction is:

The thing I like best about your paper is:

Activity 3-26

Open the database of the countries you have entered, **DB2-171, DB2-172, DB2-173,** or **DB2-174**. You will need to add two fields to the records. The fields will be percent of arable land and percent of urban population. Enter the numbers in decimal form. Work with the same group and team members that you have worked previously.

Group 1

Country	Arable land	Urban population
Belarus	.51	.67
Georgia	.15	.57
Tajikistan	.13	.65
Slovakia	.42	.69
Ukraine	.56	.68
Latvia	.27	.71
Slovenia	.22	.59
Macedonia	.29	.68
Russia	.11	.74
Azerbaijan	.10	.58
Croatia	.25	.65
Moldova	.51	.48

Save the database as **DB3-261** and print it.

EDITORIAL ASSISTANT—PART I

As the Editorial Assistant, it is your responsibility to ensure that the team works together and accomplishes its goals. Each member of the team has a responsibility. The success of the team is dependent upon each member helping other members of the team. Each paper should be checked to improve wording. The papers should also be checked for mechanics. Each person needs to complete an Editorial Assistant Evaluation I form for every paper.

You will be responsible for evaluating how well the group worked together as a team. Make sure your evaluation is accurate so that if there are any areas of weakness, they can be recognized and corrected.

Activity 3-24

Use the database on countries and work with the same team. Create a report. Show each country's name, population, and male and female life expectancies. Create a column on the report showing the difference between male and female life expectancies. Enter a title on the report, with your name on the second line of the title. Print the report. Create a second report that shows each country's name, square miles, population, and density. The density is calculated by dividing the population by the square miles. Enter a title on the report, with your name on the second line of the title. Save the last report as **DB3-241, DB3-242, DB3-243,** or **DB3-244**.

Activity 3-25

Use the database on houses, **DB2-18**. Create a database report. Show the street address, the square feet, the price, and the price per square foot. Enter your name as part of the title and print the report. Save the report as **DB3-25**.

Editorial Assistant
Evaluation I

Name: ______________________________

Team Members' Names: ______________________________

____

____

Date: ____________________

Class Period: ______________

The following applies to all members of the team
(Rank from a low of 1 to a high of 5)

Team began work quickly (1 to 5 rating) __________

Members of the team stayed together
(Number of people on the team that did not
leave the team without permission from the teacher) __________

Did not disturb other people in the room (1 to 5 rating) __________

Participation
(Number of people on the team that participated
90% or more of the time) __________

Looking at speaker
(Number of people on the team that looked at the
person speaking 70% or more of the time) __________

Eliminate "put-downs"
(Number of people on the team that did not use any put-downs) __________

Completed all evaluation forms
(Number of evaluation forms completed) __________

The thing this team did best was: __________

Activity 3-21

Open the database **DB2-18**. List all houses with two bedrooms. Print the list. List all houses with three bedrooms and two bathrooms. Print the list. List all houses with more than 1,800 square feet that cost less than $85,000. Print the list. Save the last list as **DB3-21**.

Activity 3-22

Open the database **DB2-19**. Find the record for Carolyn Schofield. List all English teachers. Print the list. List all math teachers that teach less than 125 students. Print the list. Save the last list as **DB3-22**.

Activity 3-23

Open the database with which you worked in Activity 3-20. Work with the same team. List all countries with more than 500,000 square miles. Print the list. List all countries with a male life expectancy less than 60. Print the list. List all countries with a male and female life expectancy over 65. Print the list. Save the last list as **DB3-231, DB3-232, DB3-233,** or **DB3-234**.

Activity 1-11

THE DESCRIPTIVE COMPOSITION—PART II

Now that you have written the five-sentence description, you are prepared to write a descriptive composition with more than one paragraph. Again you will be using a word processor, so you don't have to worry about getting the paper perfect the first time. In addition, you will have other people helping you with the paper so that you will not have to do all the work yourself.

It is important to remember and use the techniques that you practiced in the five-sentence description. Make use of descriptive verbs, adverbs, and adjectives. Try to include similes (comparing two unlike things) and personification (giving human qualities to things, places, or ideas) in your paper. Use proper punctuation, proper capitalization, and a variety of sentence structures.

Step 1

Write a paper of three paragraphs or more in length describing a sporting event or a play you attended. Make use of your software's spell checker, thesaurus, and Grammatik.

Save the document as **WP1-11A**.

Step 2

Incorporate in your paper your teacher's suggestions for improvement. Save the corrected document as **WP1-11B** and print a copy of the document for each team member.

Step 3

Work with members of your team to make improvements in the papers. Each team member will have specific suggestions for improvements to the papers. Don't forget to use the techniques from Activity 1-10 and also incorporate the additional ideas from this lesson. Use these techniques to develop the best paper possible for each team member.

Activity 3-20

Open the database from Activity 2-17. You should work with the same group of countries and the same team of students with which you worked in Activity 2-17. It was saved as **DB2-171, DB2-172, DB2-173,** or **DB2-174**.

Group 1

Sort the countries database so that Russia is the first country listed and Slovenia is the last country listed. Print the sorted list. Sort the database so that Macedonia is the second country listed and Ukraine is the next to last country listed. Print the sorted list. Sort the countries so that Slovakia is the third country and Croatia is the fourth country. Print the sorted list. Save the last sorted list as **DB3-201**.

Group 2

Sort the countries database so that Gambia is the first country listed and Egypt is the last country listed. Print the sorted list. Sort the database so that Chad is the second country listed and Liberia is the next to last country listed. Print the sorted list. Sort the countries so that Ghana is the sixth country and Zaire is the seventh country. Print the sorted list. Save the last sorted list as **DB3-202**.

Group 3

Sort the countries database so that India is the first country listed and Singapore is the last country listed. Print the sorted list. Sort the database so that Laos is the second country listed and Indonesia is the next to last country listed. Print the sorted list. Sort the countries so that Cambodia is the first country and South Korea is the next to last country. Print the sorted list. Save the last sorted list as **DB3-203**.

Group 4

Sort the countries database so that Panama is the first country listed and the United States is the last country listed. Print the sorted list. Sort the database so that Brazil is the second country listed and Panama is the next to last country listed. Print the sorted list. Sort the countries so that Venezuela is the seventh country and Paraguay is the eighth country. Print the sorted list. Save the last sorted list as **DB3-204**.

Step 4

Use the word processor to incorporate the suggestions gathered in Step 3 into your document. Enter the names of the team members at the bottom of your paper. Exchange papers with your other team members. Have the other members of the team check the paper before it is turned in for a grade. This can be done by viewing the document on the screen or from a hard copy of the paper. After all members of the team have checked your paper, save your document as **WP1-11** and print the document.

Activity 3-19

Open the database **DB2-19**. Sort the teacher database by degree in ascending order. Print the sorted list. Sort the database with subject as the first sort field and students as the second sort field. Sort both fields in ascending order. Save the last sorted database as **DB3-19**.

POWER WORD ADVISOR—PART II

It is important that the papers make use of descriptive verbs, adjectives, and adverbs. You may want to use the list of expressive verbs and power words for making suggestions for improvements. These words should be used to make the paper more interesting, but avoid using these words in such a way as to make the paper silly or unbelievable.

Make sure your paper includes figurative language. Try to include a simile and/or a personification. In addition, the author should use hyperbole and/or a metaphor. Hyperbole exaggerates to make a point (e.g., "The pass from the quarterback flew towards the receiver at the speed of sound."). A metaphor is much like a simile but makes the comparisons more directly. When using a metaphor you simply say something is one thing else (e.g., "The school was a highway leading to a successful and happy life.").

To make a reader feel more a part of the description, it is important to include the five senses. Using what we see, hear, smell, taste, or touch helps the reader visualize the scene and makes the description more realistic. For example, instead of just describing what a fire looks like, tell about the smell of the fire, the feel of the heat, and the sounds the fire makes.

Descriptive compositions should make use of location words, phrases, and clauses to help the reader picture the scene. This is how one item in the description is related to another in location (e.g., "The angry player towered over the referee."). Using location relationships provides elaboration to the paper to make it more accurate and interesting.

As the Power Word Advisor, it is your job to work with other members of your team to make all the papers colorful and interesting. Good descriptive papers depend on using specific details that are elaborated. Incorporate the techniques from Activity 1-10 and the additional techniques discussed in this lesson to create a powerful and effective descriptive paper. You will need to complete the evaluation form for each team member.

Database

Objectives

In this section, you will practice the following database skills:

- Sort and search databases
- Create a database report
- Add fields to a database, including a calculated field
- Create a database

In this section, you will practice the following software skills:

- Use a spreadsheet to perform calculations on data from databases
- Use a paint or draw program

In this section, you will build the following academic skills:

- Analyze or solve problems
- Work with geographical data
- Perform calculations using percentages
- Analyze or interpret graphs, charts, or maps

Activity 3-18

Open the database **DB1-16.** Sort the student database alphabetically by last name in ascending order. Sort the student database in ascending order by number of hours watched on the weekend. Sort the database with favorite type of show as the first sort field in ascending order and hours watched during the week as the second sort field in ascending order. Print the database showing the last sorted file. Save the last sorted database as **DB3-18**.

Power Word Advisor
Evaluation II

Name: ______________________________

Writer's Name: ______________________________

Date: ____________________

Class Period: ______________

The best use of expressive verbs, adjectives, and adverbs is when you describe:
Other ways to use expressive words might be:

Your best use of figurative language (simile, personification, hyperbole, or metaphor) is:

Another way you could use figurative language (simile, personification, hyperbole, or metaphor) would be:

A way you could use the five senses would be:

A few ways to use location relationships would be:

What I like best about your paper is:

Activity 3-17

Start your spreadsheet software and open file **T317**. if you are not using the template disk, open a new spreadsheet. In either case, continue with the following instructions.

Create a bar chart showing projected population by race for the year 2000. The figures given are in thousands.

White	Black	Am. Indian	Asian	Hispanic
266,108	34,642	2,383	10,991	28,693

Save the file as **SS3-17**.

MECHANICS SUPERVISOR—PART II

The Mechanics Supervisor is responsible for the paper being grammatically correct. You will need to check the team members' papers for proper spelling, capitalization, punctuation, and sentence structure. In addition, check the papers for correct subject-verb agreement, correct verb tense and verb forms, correct pronouns, and other English usage.

Make sure if the author is using a singular form of a noun or pronoun, that a singular verb is also used (e.g., "Pat and Alice believes the story Terri wrote."). This would be incorrect because the plural *believe* should be used instead of *believes.*

If the author is writing in the past tense, it is important that a past tense verb is used (e.g., "Last week we hike in Big Ben National Park" is incorrect). The past tense of *hike* (*hiked*) should be used. Irregular verbs for the past and past participle are formed in different ways than regular verbs (e.g., "The light has shined for three days."). In this sentence, *shone* should be used instead of *shined.*

Make sure the author is using the correct pronoun form.

Correct	Incorrect
I looked at the dragon and its eyes were red.	I looked at the dragon and it's eyes were red.
Greg and I went to the car show.	Greg and me went to the car show.
The teacher complimented her and me.	The teacher complimented she and I.

When using pronouns, most of the problems occur when there are compound subjects or objects. If you try the sentence using just one subject or object, it is usually easier to determine the correct pronoun. For example, you know you would not say, "Me went to a car show" or "The teacher complimented I."

It will be your job to recognize and use appropriate English usage within your team members' compositions. Be sure to review the instructions from the Mechanics Supervisor Part I work sheet (Activity 1-10). You will need to complete the Mechanics Supervisor evaluation form for each member of the team, including yourself.

Activity 3-15

Start your spreadsheet software and open file **T315**. If you are not using the template disk, open a new spreadsheet. In either case, continue with the following instructions.

Create a pie chart showing the distribution of microcomputers in U.S. schools. Enter a title on the chart and make sure the chart is properly labeled. The figures are given in thousands.

Elementary	Middle Grades	High School
897	583	895

Save the file as **SS3-15** and print it.

Activity 3-16

For the years 1989 to 1992, create a line chart comparing the value of new vehicles imported from Japan to the value of new cars exported to Japan.

Value of new cars (given in millions of dollars) imported from Japan from 1989 to 1992.

1989	1990	1991	1992
19,912	19,220	20,422	20,538

Value of new cars (given in millions of dollars) exported to Japan from 1989 to 1992.

1989	1990	1991	1992
327	531	496	694

Save the file as **SS3-16** and print it.

Mechanics Supervisor
Evaluation II

Name: ____

Writer's Name: ____

Date: __________________________

Class Period: ___________________

Spelling, punctuation, or capitalization errors that need correction are:

A good example of a compound, complex, or compound-complex sentence in your paper is:

A way you might combine or reword sentences to have greater variety or clarity would be:

English usage mistakes that need correction are:

The thing I like best about your paper is:

Objectives

In this section, you will practice the following spreadsheet skills:
- Create a pie chart
- Create a line chart
- Create a bar chart

In this section, you will build the following academic skills:
- Express data using charts or graphs
- Compare data using charts or graphs

Activity 3-14

Create a pie chart to show the sales by department for a clothing store.

Men's	25,000
Women's	56,000
Juniors'	70,000
Children's	34,000

Save the spreadsheet as **SS3-14**.

EDITORIAL ASSISTANT—PART II

You will need to make sure the evaluations are completed by the Power Word Advisor and the Mechanics Supervisor. As the Editorial Assistant, you will also need to check the overall composition of the paper. Be sure the ideas and techniques used in Activity 1-10 are included in each paragraph of the composition for Activity 1-11. You will need to make sure the paper is well-organized and communicates effectively as a whole.

The opening paragraph must describe the whole scene. Parts of the scene should be divided into the paragraphs that make up the body of the composition. For example, if the composition is describing a basketball game, one paragraph might describe the crowd, another the players, a third the cheerleaders, and a fourth the band. Each paragraph should use powerful images and figurative language in a variety of sentence structures to describe a particular aspect of the scene. The scene should be described in a logical order. The use of the five senses should be included to make the paper more vivid and realistic. The closing paragraph should be much like the first paragraph. The ending paragraph repeats the ideas of the first paragraph without repeating the words exactly.

Finally, check the basic format of the document. Determine if the document has the correct heading and is ready to print.

You will also be responsible for evaluating how well the group worked together as a team. Keep in mind that the evaluation for teamwork does not apply to a particular individual but to the entire team.

Teamwork Checklist

Began work on time

Team stayed on task

Was considerate of other teams in the room

All team members treated with respect

Editorial Assistant
Evaluation II

Name: ______________________________

Writer's Name: ______________________________

Date: __________________

Class Period: _____________

Why would you say the paper is well organized?

Improvements that could be made to the paper's organization:

The best examples of elaboration are:

A way you could elaborate more might be:

Corrections needed in the format of the document:

The Team:

Started on time and stayed on task (Rank from a low of 1 to a high of 5):

Treated each other and other class members with respect (1 to 5 rating):

Number of people on team that participated 90% or more of the time:

Elaboration Checklist

Use of descriptive adjectives and adverbs

Good use of action verbs

Figurative language:
Simile
Metaphor
Personification
Hyperbole

Use of five senses

Mechanics Checklist

Correct spelling

Correct punctuation

Correct capitalization

Correct subject-verb agreement

Correct use of pronouns

Sentence Checklist

No sentence fragments or run-on sentences

Good topic sentences

Good use of transitional sentences and phrases

Objectives

In this section, you will practice the following database skills:

- Plan, create, and save a database
- Enter data in records

In this section, you will build the following academic skills:

- Work with geographical data
- Use customary and metric measurements
- Work with astronomical data
- Solve problems involving percents
- Solve problems involving fractions

Activity 1-12

Open your database software and create a database for one of the following groups of countries. The database will have four fields. The Square Miles and Population fields will be numeric fields. Make certain that field widths are large enough to handle the biggest entry.

Group 1

Country	Square Miles	Population	Capital
Belarus	80,154	10,200,000	Minsk
Georgia	26,911	5,449,000	Tbilisi
Tajikistan	55,251	5,112,000	Dushanbe
Slovakia	18,924	4,991,168	Bratislava
Ukraine	233,089	51,704,000	Kiev
Latvia	24,595	2,681,000	Riga
Slovenia	7,898	1,891,864	Ljubljana
Macedonia	9,889	1,909,136	Skopje
Russia	6,592,812	147,386,000	Moscow
Azerbaijan	33,436	7,029,000	Baku
Croatia	22,050	4,601,470	Zagreb
Moldova	13,102	4,341,000	Kishinev

Save the file as **DB1-121**. Close the file.

with two members, you will write the opening and second paragraph of your paper and the third and closing paragraph of your team member's paper. At the bottom of the paper, enter the names of the team members and which paragraphs each member wrote.

For example:

Team member A selects the best ideas from the brainstorming session and writes the opening paragraph of A's composition. Team member A then moves to the computer of team member B and writes the second paragraph of B's composition. The second paragraph tells how the subjects of the composition are alike. Team member A then moves to the word processor of team member C and writes the third paragraph for C's composition. This paragraph tells how the subjects of the composition are different. Team member A then moves back to A's computer and writes A's closing paragraph. The opening paragraph becomes very important because each team member will be using it as a guide for writing subsequent paragraphs.

When working on a team member's paper, you may use the list of brainstorming ideas selected by the writer of the paper. It will be important, when writing a paragraph for each paper, to maintain consistency in the document. Paragraphs in the body of the composition should reflect ideas from the opening paragraph.

Step 4

After each composition is complete, each team member will have specific items to check on each document. On the first paper, you will check the elaboration, on the second paper you will check the mechanics, and on the third paper you will check the sentence structure and transitional sentences. At the bottom of the paper, list which team member checked elaboration, mechanics, and sentences. Also indicate which team member wrote each paragraph.

All team members will fill out a portion of the evaluation sheet on teamwork. On two-member teams, one member will check elaboration and the other will check transitional sentences and combining sentences. Both team members will check mechanics and teamwork.

Checklists are provided on pages 136–137 to show what to look for on the papers you will be evaluating.

Group 2

Country	Square Miles	Population	Capital
Uganda	91,076	18,690,000	Kampala
Gambia	4,127	875,000	Banjul
Algeria	919,591	26,022,000	Algiers
Zimbabwe	150,803	10,720,000	Harare
Ghana	92,099	15,617,700	Accra
Liberia	43,000	2,730,000	Monrovia
South Africa	455,318	40,601,000	Cape Town; Pretoria
Mozambique	303,769	15,113,000	Maputo
Zaire	290,585	8,446,000	Kinshasa
Egypt	386,659	54,452,000	Cairo
Ethiopia	426,366	50,576,300	Addis Ababa
Chad	495,752	5,122,000	N'Djamena

Save the file as **DB1-122**. Close the file.

Group 3

Country	Square Miles	Population	Capital
Cambodia	69,898	7,146,000	Phnom Penh
Indonesia	788,430	193,560,000	Jakarta
Iran	636,293	59,051,000	Tehran
India	1,269,339	869,515,000	New Delhi
Vietnam	128,405	67,568,000	Hanoi
Philippines	115,707	65,759,000	Manila
North Korea	46,540	21,815,000	Pyongyang
Laos	91,428	4,113,000	Vientiane
Myanmar	261,789	42,112,000	Rangoon
Bangladesh	55,126	116,601,000	Dhaka
South Korea	38,175	43,134,000	Seoul
Singapore	226	2,756,000	Singapore

Save the file as **DB1-123**. Close the file.

Activity 3-13

THE COMPARATIVE COMPOSITION—PART II

Work with the same team with which you worked in Activity 3-12. Write a comparative composition of four paragraphs in length. Incorporate the techniques used in the five-sentence paragraph. Each paragraph should begin with a topic sentence and the composition should be well-organized.

Step 1

Select a topic from one of the following choices:

English class and math class

Male teachers and female teachers

Living in a small town and living in a large city

Elementary school and middle school

Two different states in the U.S.

The Civil War and World War II

Home of one of your grandparents and your home

Each team member should select a different topic.

After each person has selected a topic, use brainstorming to put information into categories. Taking one person's topic at a time, team members should think of similarities and differences. The writer of the paper should list the similarities and the differences. After the team members feel they have exhausted the possibilities of one topic, they should move to the topic selected by another team member.

Step 2

Take notes from the teacher lecture.

Step 3

Each team member will have the responsibility of writing a portion of the composition. You will write the opening paragraph of the topic you have selected. Another team member will write the second paragraph and another team member will write the third paragraph. You will then write your closing paragraph. For teams

Group 4

Country	Square Miles	Population	Capital
Argentina	1,072,070	32,664,000	Buenos Aires
Nicaragua	45,698	3,752,000	Managua
Panama	29,761	2,476,000	Panama
Paraguay	157,047	4,799,000	Asuncion
Venezuela	352,143	20,189,000	Caracas
Brazil	3,284,426	155,356,000	Brasilia
United States	3,623,420	252,502,000	Washington, D.C.
Jamaica	56,275	2,787,424	Kingston
Haiti	10,694	6,287,000	Port-au-Prince
Cuba	44,206	10,732,000	Havana
Honduras	43,277	4,949,000	Tegucigalpa
Colombia	439,513	33,778,000	Bogota

Save the file as **DB1-124**. Close the file.

Step 4

Incorporate the suggestions from the teacher lecture in your paragraph. Each sentence should have a specific purpose. Select the best ideas from your brainstorming session to use in your paper.

After you have entered the paragraph, let other team members proofread the document on the screen.

Starting four lines under the paragraph, tab to the middle of the paper, list the team members and print your document. Save the document as **WP3-12**.

Activity 1-13

Create a new database using the following information. The database will contain five fields. Since the Address field contains both numbers and characters, it should be a character or text field. The remaining fields should be numeric fields.

Address	Bedrooms	Bathrooms	Square Feet	Price
1409 Holley	4	2.5	1,990	80,000
418 Ellis	2	1	1,450	55,000
1226 Powers	4	2.5	2,500	160,000
78 King Blvd.	3	2	1,700	48,000
1920 Jester	3	2	1,850	75,000
555 Travis	2	1	1,500	63,000
19 W. Coy	3	2	1,920	73,000
8080 Python	3	2.5	2,200	99,000

Save the database as **DB1-13**. Close the file.

Activity 3-12

THE COMPARATIVE COMPOSITION—PART I

You will be working with a team to write a comparative composition. This type of paper will compare and contrast two different items: the advantages and disadvantages of doing something, or their good and bad points. You might compare two different fast food places, the advantages and disadvantages of being in a band or on a sports team, or the good and bad points of having brothers and sisters.

Step 1

Write a five-sentence comparative paragraph on one of the following:

A word processor and a typewriter

Football and basketball

Summer and spring

Cars 30 years ago and today's cars

Russia and the United States

Each member of the team should select a different topic. After the paragraph is complete, enter your name, the date, and your class period flush right at the top of the document.

Save the document as **WP3-121**.

Step 2

Take notes from the teacher lecture on how to improve the paragraph.

Step 3

Use brainstorming and work with other members of your team to discover the ways the things or the subjects of each paragraph are similar and how they are different. Follow your teacher's instructions and list the suggestions made by your team members concerning how the subjects of your paper are alike and different. In brainstorming it is important not to criticize the ideas suggested, but write them all down. The writer of the composition can go back later and select the best suggestions.

Activity 1-14

Create a database using the following information:

Teacher Name	Degree	Subject	Building	Students
Janice Early	MS	Math	C	120
Shawna Tankersley	BS	Math	C	130
Susan Ellis	BS	Math	C	100
Katie Craddock	MS	Eng	A	140
Chalna Trawick	MS	Eng	A	130
Gwen Green	BS	Eng	A	145
Carolyn Schofield	MS	Sci	D	140
Rick McDaniel	BS	Sci	D	100

Save the database as **DB1-14**. Close the file.

Activity 3-11

CAPITALIZATION RULES

Start your word processing software and open file **T311**. If you are not using the template disk, open a new word processing document.

Enter the following capitalization rules. Use the indent and hanging indent functions of the word processor you are using.

1. Capitalize special titles when they immediately precede a personal name.

2. Capitalize the names of all nationalities, races, and tribes and the adjectives derived from them.

3. Do not capitalize north, south, east and west when they refer to a direction or a section of a state.

4. Capitalize the names of political parties and religious denominations and their members.

5. Capitalize the first word of a direct quotation.

6. Capitalize words that show family relationships when they are used instead of a name or as part of a name. Do not capitalize these words when they are preceded by a possessive such as *my*, *your*, *their*.

After each rule has been entered, double-space and key a sentence with an example of the rule.

Save the document as **WP3-11** and print it.

Activity 1-15

Create a database in which to place information on measurements. In field 1 will be the unit of measurement. In fields 2 and 3 will be equivalent measurements. In field 4 will be the conversion factor to another system of measurement.

Unit of Measurement	Equivalent 1	Equivalent 2	Conversion
1 inch	.083 feet	.027 yards	2.54 cm
1 foot	12 inches	.333 yards	.304 meters
1 meter	100 cm	.001 kilometer	39.37 inches
1 mile	5,280 feet	1,760 yards	1.609 kilometers
1 kilometer	1,000 meters	100,000 cm	.621 miles
1 furlong	660 feet	1/8 mile	201.168 meters
1 nautical mile	1.151 statute miles	2,025.76 yards	1.852 kilometers
1 ounce	1/8 cup	1/128 gallon	29.574 milliliters
1 cup	8 fluid ounces	1/2 pint	236.592 milliliters
1 gallon	8 pints	16 cups	3.785 liters
1 cubic foot	1,728 cubic inches	.037 cubic yards	.028 cubic meters
1 cubic yard	48,655 cubic inches	27 cubic feet	.028316 cubic meters

Column headings should align with column data or be centered.

Save the database as **DB1-15**. Close the file.

Activity 3-10

SERVICE TECHNICIAN

Enter the following questions in the format shown. Use the indent or hanging indent function of the word processor you are using. Use **WP1-02** to answer the questions. Underline the correct answer.

1. Which is the best main idea for the article?

   a. The computer service technician maintains and repairs equipment.
   b. A computer service technician should be able to read and understand manuals.
   c. A computer service technician should be able to think logically.
   d. A computer service technician does not need to know how to type.

2. Which is a detail in the article?

   a. Technicians work mostly at night when the people who use the computers have gone home.
   b. The only place to learn computer repair is in college.
   c. Manufacturers constantly improve their machines.
   d. Computers run for years by themselves without repair or service.

3. Which of these is in correct sequence (time order), according to the article?

   a. Many technicians first learn to repair electric typewriters.
   b. Computer repair is always needed after a thunderstorm.
   c. After basic training, a technician will be able to work on any computer ever invented.
   d. The technician must find the problem before repairing a computer.

Save the document as **WP3-10** and print it.

Activity 1-16

You have been asked to set up a database with information on the planets. The database should contain the following information: planet name, closest distance to the sun, greatest distance from the sun, diameter of the planet, density, and gravity. The distances and diameters are given in miles.

	A	B	C	D	E
Earth	91,400,000	94,500,000	7,927	5.520	100%
Jupiter	460,000,000	507,000,000	88,700	1.310	287%
Mars	128,500,000	154,900,000	4,200	3.950	38%
Mercury	28,600,000	43,000,000	3,031	5.440	38%
Neptune	2,754,000,000	2,821,000,000	30,200	1.660	123%
Pluto	2,748,000,000	4,571,200,000	1,900	1.000	3%
Saturn	838,000,000	932,000,000	74,600	0.704	132%
Uranus	1,700,000,000	1,860,000,000	31,570	1.210	93%
Venus	66,800,000	67,700,000	7,520	5.270	90%

A – Closest distance to the sun
B – Greatest distance from the sun
C – Diameter of the planet
D – Density
E – Gravity (in relation to Earth)

Save the database as **DB1-16**. Close the file.

3. Which of these is in correct sequence (time order), according to the article?

   a. Before being employed, the analyst must have at least a bachelor's degree.
   b. After the system is designed, the analyst never goes back to that office again.
   c. Before the system is designed, the analyst learns about the company, the needs, the equipment, and the people who will be using it.
   d. Good analysts develop their own systems and sell them to all their customers.

Activity 1-17

Build a database using the following clues. The database should contain fields for the person's name, department, years of experience with the company, age, and hourly pay.

Hilda has eight years' experience and works in the Shipping Department.

Jerry is 31 and earns $8 per hour.

Shalandra has five years' experience.

Hilda is 41.

Hector is 35 and makes $10 per hour.

Rieko has five years' experience and is 27.

Marsha makes $14 per hour.

Jerry has twice as much experience as Shalandra and Reiko.

The people in the Accounting Department earn the same hourly pay.

Jerry is paid two-thirds as much as Rieko.

Two people work in the Marketing Department.

People working in Shipping make 80 percent of the pay of people working in Accounting.

Shalandra was 28 when she began working for the company.

There are an equal number of employees in each department.

Jerry is ten years younger than Hilda, who is older than Reiko.

Reiko and Marsha work in the same department.

Hilda, Hector, and Marsha have the same number years of experience.

Jerry does not work in the same department as Shalandra and Hector.

Shalandra works in the Accounting Department.

Take the square root of 81. Multiply it by 4. That is Marsha's age. The square root of 81 is also the difference between the ages of Marsha and Rieko.

The total years' experience of all employees is 44.

The average pay for all employees is $10.33 per hour.

The average age of the employees is 33.83 years.

Save the database as **DB1-17**. Close the file.

Activity 3-9

SYSTEMS ANALYST

Start your word processing software and open file **T309**. If you are not using the template disk, open a new word processing document.

Enter the following questions and answers concerning document **WP1-05**. Boldface the correct answers. Save the document as **WP3-09** and print it.

1. The author of this passage gives you enough evidence to believe that ___

   a. every student should go to college.
   b. the only good jobs in the future will be computer jobs.
   c. systems analysts should not operate their own businesses.
   d. a person who is skilled in using computers and willing to learn might like a job as a systems analyst.

2. Which is a correct statement of cause and effect, according to the article?

   a. Because the analyst has talked to several people, considered their needs, and designed a suitable program, the systems analyst is really knowledgeable about an office's system.
   b. Because the analyst knows much about an office, that person's background must be checked carefully to be sure the analyst is not a spy.
   c. Because of access to a great deal of company secrets, an analyst can make a lot of money selling corporate secrets to other companies.
   d. Because they know computers well, all analysts are more intelligent than all secretaries.

Activity 1-18

Design a survey to find television habits of the students in your class. Determine the number of hours students watch television and the type of shows they watch, such as soaps, situation comedies, sports, music videos, etc. The survey should ask for the students' favorite shows. The survey should determine the number of hours the person watches TV during the week and the number of hours they watch on the weekend. Use a word processor to key the survey. Place the results of the survey in a database. Enter the students' names, last name first. The fields should contain the following information:

Student name
Favorite type of show
Favorite show
Hours of TV watched during the week
Hours of TV watched on the weekend

Save the database as **DB1-18**.

Change the font of the correct answer in Question 4 to any other font.

Enter your name and the current date in a footer. Preview and print the document. Save the document as **WP3-08** and print it.

Objectives

In this section you will practice the following spreadsheet skills:

- Open a spreadsheet
- Enter values and text in a spreadsheet
- Save a spreadsheet

In this section, you will build the following academic skills:

- Find squares and square roots
- Demonstrate an understanding of mathematical relations and functions
- Apply geometric properties
- Demonstrate an understanding of measurement concepts using metric and customary units
- Analyze or solve problems

Activity 1-19

MEASUREMENT

Start your spreadsheet software and open file **T119**. If you are not using the template disk, open a new spreadsheet. In either case, continued with the following instructions.

In measurement problems, you are often asked to convert from one unit of measurement to another. For example, you might be asked to convert from gallons to quarts or from meters to kilometers. If you are going from a large unit of measurement (such as a gallon) to a smaller one (such as a quart), you must multiply by the conversion factor. Since there are four quarts in a gallon, the conversion factor is four.

If you are going from a smaller measurement (such as a meter) to a larger one (such as a kilometer), you would divide by the conversion factor. There are 1,000 meters in a kilometer. To determine the number of kilometers in 8,000 meters, you would divide 8,000 by 1,000.

Set up spreadsheets to perform the following calculations. Format output to two decimal places. You may place the spreadsheets in one file.

Activity 3-8

Enter the following questions and answers. Use indents and tabs.

1. If an average person produces six pounds of trash per day, and 2/5 of the trash is paper, how much paper does the average person throw away in a day?

    a. 4 pounds   c. 40 pounds
    b. 2.4 pounds   d. 24 pounds

2. If you place a stack of newspapers with the dimensions of 4 feet x 1 foot x 1.2 feet in the trash, how many cubic feet would the stack be?

    a. 4.8 cubic feet   c. 6.2 cubic feet
    b. 8.8 cubic feet   d. 48 cubic inches

3. If 20 families each placed 4.8 cubic feet of newspapers in the trash every week, how many cubic feet of waste in newspapers do they create in a year?

    a. 96 cubic feet   c. 1,152 cubic feet
    b. 11,520 cubic feet   d. 4,992 cubic feet

4. If 100 families each place 5 cubic feet of newspapers each week in a classroom that is 20 feet long, 25 feet wide, and 10 feet tall, how long would it take to fill the classroom?

    a. 10 weeks   c. 50 weeks
    b. 25 weeks   d. 1 week

Underline the correct answer in Question 1.

Boldface the correct answer in Question 2.

Italicize the correct answer in Question 3.

1. Convert the following kilometers to miles.

	A	B
1	Kilometers	Miles
2	8	
3	12.8	
4	19.21	
5	35.1	

Convert the following miles to kilometers.

	A	B
7	Miles	Kilometers
8	15	
9	34	
10	8	
11	26	

2. Sarah works for Garza Petro. Mr. Garza has several containers of kerosene in the warehouse. He wants to find out how many quarts of kerosene he has. He has the following containers of kerosene. How many total quarts of kerosene does he have in stock?

10 gallons	12 pints	4 gallons
6 gallons	3 pints	6 pints
8 pints	18 gallons	11 pints

3. A customer comes into Hilson Hardware to buy string to mark plots of land. He will need enough string to mark four lots. How many centimeters of string will he need for each lot and how many total centimeters of string will he need? He wants the string to go around the perimeter of the following size lots.

8. What is a LAN?
   a. Laptops And News
   b. Low Analog Netting
   c. Local Area Network
   d. Limited Approach Netting

Length	Width
39 meters	40 meters
22 meters	40 meters
46 meters	54 meters
50 meters	32 meters

4. Convert the following measurements to feet and add each row. Format the answer to one decimal place.

Miles	Yards	Inches
2.0	12.0	24
2.2	1.5	36
3.10	40.0	36
4.0	80.0	48
3.5	20.0	12
2.6	10.3	72

5. David's Ice Cream Shoppe has five part-time employees. The following are the names and the number of hours each worked for a three-day period. They are each paid $4.50 per hour. Calculate the total number of hours each employee worked and the gross pay for each.

Name	Wednesday	Thursday	Friday
Cherrie	3 hr. 20 min.	4 hr. 10 min.	7 hr. 20 min.
Holli	4 hr. 15 min.	3 hr. 40 min.	6 hr. 45 min.
Staci	4 hr. 40 min.	4 hr. 50 min.	7 hr. 30 min.
Pam	3 hr. 45 min.	5 hr. 10 min.	7 hr. 45 min.
Juanita	5 hr. 10 min.	3 hr. 45 min.	6 hr. 50 min.

2. Component means
   a. an individual part
   b. a computer system
   c. a network system
   d. several parts

3. Vendor means
   a. a buyer
   b. a seller
   c. a machine
   d. a computer technician

4. Internally means
   a. within the company
   b. inside the computer
   c. from other countries
   d. inexpensively

5. Prioritize means
   a. cut expenses
   b. save money
   c. not make a firm decision
   d. place things in order of importance

6. Documentation means
   a. individualized training
   b. group training
   c. written instructions
   d. a written warranty or guarantee

7. Forefront means
   a. a dangerous position
   b. before others
   c. in the majority
   d. a top position or job

6. Measure the top of the desk or table at which you sit. Measure the length and width of the top. Also measure the distance from the top front of the desk to the floor. Make the measurements in inches. After the measurements are taken and recorded on a spreadsheet, convert the measurements to feet and then convert the measurements to yards.

Save and print the file as **SS1-19**.

Activity 3-7

Read the following passage:

LANs (Local Area Networks)

There is a great deal to chose from when considering LANs. The possible number of network configurations is somewhere between boundless and infinite. Buying a LAN is somewhat like buying a jigsaw puzzle one piece at a time. In most cases you must buy each component separately.

When buying a LAN, service and support must be discussed up front with the vendor or consultant. Some companies want to provide support internally, but you should get a small amount of training and support from the vendor.

Because the network will service a local area, such as one location, planning should start with viewing the company's goals. You will need to prioritize. Because having everything you want in a local network can be expensive, decisions must be made as to the degree of importance of desired objectives.

When deciding on whom to buy from, it is important to examine each vendor's track record. It is also critical to receive adequate documentation with the network. Trying to figure out how the network works and how to correct problems can be very frustrating with no written manuals.

Buying a LAN is a major decision. With proper planning and careful study you will find yourself on the forefront of an exciting field. However, it may be a lonely position to lead the pack.

Start your word processing software and open the file **T307**. If you are not using the template disk, open a new word processing document.

Enter the following questions. Without using a dictionary, boldface the correct definition. Save the document as **WP3-07** and print it.

```
1.  Infinite means
    a. A long passage of time
    b. Lasting forever
    c. An endless number
    d. Limited in number
```

Activity 1-20

AVERAGE

There are three measures of central tendency: mean, median, and mode. You will be working with all three in this activity.

Average or Mean

Average is calculated by adding a group of numbers together and dividing the total by the number of pieces of data. Another word for average is **arithmetic mean** or **mean.** A student's grade average is an example of the mean. A grade is determined by adding all the grades together and dividing by the number of grades.

Median

Another measure of central tendency is the median. The median is the middle numeral of a set of numerals that are placed in order. If there is an even number of numerals, you get the average of the middle two numerals. If you had the numerals 10, 8, 12, 6, and 4, you would first place them in order. For example:

4 6 8 10 12

The middle numeral, or median, is 8.

Mode

A third measure of central tendency is mode. Mode is the number appearing most often in a series of numbers. For example:

6 7 12 7 6 20 14 7

Seven is the mode because it is the number appearing most often.

Finding the Missing Number

You may be given a problem in which the average is given and all the data is given except for one number. You are required to determine the missing number.

For example: The average high temperature for the first five days in February was 33. The high temperatures for the first four days were 30, 29, 34, and 31. What was the high temperature for the fifth day?

Activity 3-6

Key the following information on the countries shown as a table or use columns to properly align all items. Arrange in order of GDP rank, first through sixth. Label four columns as Country, GDP (in millions of dollars), GDP Rank, and Population (in millions).

Enter *Prepared By:* and your name at the bottom of the document and print the document. Save the document as **WP3-06**.

Japan–ranked first in Gross Domestic Product with $2,302,600 million–has 125 million people.

Myanmar ranks just above Uganda, fifth. It has a $22,200 million GDP and 43 million people.

Second in rank is France: $1,100,300 million GDP and 58 million in population.

Canada is third. Its Gross Domestic Product is $521,300 million. It has 27 million people.

With a GDP of $28,500 million, Nigeria is fourth on the list. Nigeria has 89 million people

Uganda has a population of 19 million, and its GDP is $5,600 million.

Step 1

To solve this problem, first add the data you are given.

$$\begin{array}{r} 30 \\ 29 \\ 34 \\ \underline{31} \\ 124 \end{array}$$

Step 2

Multiply the average times the number of days involved.

33 x 5 = 165

Be sure to multiply the average times a number that is one greater than the number of data given. There are four numbers given, but you are working with the average of five numbers.

Step 3

Subtract the result of Step 1, from the result of Step 2.

165 – 124 = 41

Solve the following problems dealing with central tendency. You may place all the problems in the same spreadsheet file.

1. The McDonald family enjoys camping during the summer months. They always keep a record to compare daily rates of various campgrounds. Calculate the daily rate of each of the following campgrounds and the average daily rate paid by the McDonalds. The average daily rate is the average of the Daily Rate column. The first daily rate (D3) has already been calculated as an example. Format your answers to two decimal places.

Activity 3-5

1. In this activity, you will take information and create a table. The table will have three columns: name, identification number, and hourly pay. Place a heading over each column. All identification numbers, names, and hour pay amounts should be entered in the same format. Use decimal tabs to align hourly pay. Use the following information for the table.

```
Tommy C Bounds, IN 005-44-5787, $5.00 per hour.
Smith, Sally Ann, 987-65-4321, $4.75 per hour.
Cissy L. Landers, Identification Number 888-44-1515, $6
Anderson, Tony, 999-88-7777, $7.50
Cameron G. Jackson, 755-14-8989, $4.89
```

2. Enter your name, date, and class period flush right at the top of the document.

3. Print the document.

4. Save the document as **WP3-05**.

	A	B	C	D
1			Total	Daily
2	Camp	Days	Cost	Rate
3	Lake of the Pines	5	75.00	15.00
4	Cedar Creek Lake	7	126.00	
5	Toledo Bend Lake	6	75.00	
6	Lake Bonham	7	84.00	
7	Lake Ray Hubbard	3	48.00	
8				
9			Avg Daily	

2. The following are the names and scores of the top ten students from the last math test. Find (a) the mean score, (b) the median for the scores, and (c) the mode for the scores. You may not be able to use spreadsheet functions to find all of the answers.

Name	**Grade**
Wyatt	94
Gayla	90
Michelle	100
Jason	100
Megan	98
Misty	98
James	92
Angelique	96
Julie	94
Norma Jean	98
David	96

3. Juan, the leading basketball player last year, scored an average of 24 points a game. This year Toby has scored the following points in the first five games: 22, 24, 22, 26, and 24. What must he score in the final game to tie Juan's average?

Activity 3-4

Enter the following. Check in your word processing user's manual to see how to enter special characters such as pi (π) and how to superscript and subscript numbers. On the superscripted and subscripted numbers, use a smaller point size. Boldface the name of the formulas.

Perimeter	square	P = 4s
	rectangle	P = 2*(l+w)
Circumference	circle	C = 2πr
Area	square	A = s^2
	rectangle	A = l*w
	triangle	A = (b*h)/2
	trapezoid	A = $\frac{1}{2}(b_1 + b_2)h$
	circle	A = πr^2
Surface	cube	S = $6s^2$
Volume	rectangular prism	V = lwh
	cylinder	V = $\pi r^2 h$
	cube	V = s^3
Pythagorean theorem	right triangle	$c^2 = a^2 + b^2$

In the formulas, *r* is radius, *s* is side, *l* is length, and *h* is height. In calculations, you can use 3.14 for pi (π).

Preview and print the document. You may need to double-space the document. Save the document as **WP3-04**.

4. You will need to work with two or three other students to conduct an experiment. You are going to conduct a study of the speed of reaction of four students in your class. For the study you will need a yardstick. Have each of the students hold out their hands, thumbs up, one foot apart. One at a time, hold a yardstick above each student's head. When you drop the yardstick, the students should bring their hands together to catch the stick. Write down the number on the yardstick where the students' forefingers meet. Use a spreadsheet to determine the mean, median, and mode of where the four students' forefingers met. Compare your findings with other teams in the room. Find the mean, median, and mode for all the students in the class. You may not be able to use spreadsheet functions to find all of the answers.

Save the file as **SS1-20**.

Activity 3-3

Set tabs for three columns to show the authors, time periods, and their works. In the first column place the author's name, in the next column place the time period, and in the third column place a work of the author. After the columns are complete, make sure your name is on the document and print it. Save the document as **WP3-03**.

Author
Shakespeare
Shelley
Dickens
Darwin
Hardy
Spenser
Bunyan
Swift
Kipling
Stevenson
Conrad
Wolfe
Scott

Time Period
Later Victorian
Later Victorian
Later Victorian
Later Victorian
Romantic
Romantic
Victorian
Victorian
Elizabethan
Elizabethan
Age of Reason
Puritan
20th Century

Work
As You Like It
Look Homeward Angel
Treasure Island
Gulliver's Travels
The Faerie Queene
Pilgrims Progress
The Origin of Species
To a Skylark
Gunga Din
A Tale of Two Cities
Jude the Obscure
Lord Jim
Ivanhoe

Activity 1-21

EXPONENTIAL NUMBERS AND SQUARE ROOTS

Start your spreadsheet software and open file **T121**. If you are not using the template disk, open a new spreadsheet. In either case, continue with the following instructions.

You will be solving problems dealing with exponential numbers and square roots. The spreadsheet software you are using is capable of performing these calculations very quickly and accurately. The software has a function to calculate square roots. For example, in Lotus® 1-2-3®, to determine the square root of 12 you would enter @SQRT(12). If you are using WordPerfect® Works the function is =SQRT(12). Determine the function for calculating square roots for the software you are using.

The square of a number can be calculated by using the caret (^). For example, to calculate 3^2, you would key 3^2 in the cell in the spreadsheet.

Always be aware of the order of operations. The program will first perform any calculations involving exponential numbers, such as squares. The program will then perform calculations for multiplication and division and finally for addition and subtraction. Parentheses can be used to change the order of operations.

In the problem $4 + 3 * 2^2$, the answer is 16. The program will first square 2, then multiply the result by 3, and then add 4. If you want to add the 3 and 4 together to multiply the sum by 2 squared, you would place 4 + 3 in parentheses, i.e., $(4+3)* 2^2$. The result of this problem would be 28.

Estimating Square Roots

The key to estimating square roots is memorizing the squares from 1 to 13. Once you memorize the squares, you will know the square roots. For example, if you know that the square of 11 is 121, you know that the square root of 121 is 11. Listed below are the squares of 1 to 13.

$1^2 = 1$	$6^2 = 36$	$11^2 = 121$
$2^2 = 4$	$7^2 = 49$	$12^2 = 144$
$3^2 = 9$	$8^2 = 64$	$13^2 = 169$
$4^2 = 16$	$9^2 = 81$	
$5^2 = 25$	$10^2 = 100$	

Activity 3-2

Set tabs for three columns on the document. In the first column you will enter the following adjectives and adverbs:

```
bad
far
good
ill
little (adverb)
many
much
```

In the next column, enter the comparative of the adjective or adverb. The comparative is the form of the word when two items are being compared (e.g., Fred was taller than Bill). *Taller* is the comparative of tall.

In the third column, enter the superlative of the word. The superlative is the form of the word when more than two items are being compared (e.g., Jane is the tallest girl in the class). *Tallest* is the superlative of tall.

You can select the correct answer from the list below. Some words are used more than once, while others are incorrect and should not be used.

better
lest
less
lessor
least
more
morer
morest
best
worser
worst
worse
most
farther
further
farthest
furthest

Enter your name on the document and save it as **WP3-02**.

Once these squares are memorized and you know the square roots, you will be able to recognize if an answer is reasonable. For example, if you are asked to find the square root of 95 and your answer is 15, you will know that is not a reasonable answer. The square root of 100 is 10 and the square root of 81 is 9. Therefore, the square root of 95 must be a number between 9 and 10.

You can save the following problems in the same spreadsheet file.

1. Use the spreadsheet to calculate the square root of the following numbers. In column B, put your estimate (with two decimal places) of the square root of each number. After your estimate has been entered, place in column C the function of your spreadsheet that calculates the square root. Format your answer to three decimal places. Calculate the difference between your answer and the actual answer and find the average difference.

	A	B	C
1	Number	Estimate	Square Root
2	18		
3	135		
4	70		
5	150		
6	20		
7	57		
8	118		
9	45		

2. Calculate the square of the following numbers:

5	32
10	44
1	57
20	63
25	78

Format your answer with commas.

Expressive Verbs

meander	pry	weep	implore
pace	ply	beam	recite
hike	free	lament	ponder
roam	thrust	bewail	utter
vacate	wedge	twinkle	warble
wander	hoist	snooze	coax
soar	heave	slumber	jingle
sneak	lash	counsel	ripple
descend	litter	eye	whet
stagger	warp	gaze	pardon
intrude	creak	survey	regulate
leap	refresh	endure	dominate
thrash	assign	aspire	strangle
rove	thwart	feign	rectify
nudge	slash	pledge	afflict
grasp	tear	reprove	chuckle
submerge	thrill	entreat	tilt
hurl	reform	doze	gossip
whirl	crave	assail	endeavor
grind	escort	slope	confuse
attribute	analyze	appease	join
rotate	mend	affix	frolic
swallow	flog	lash	roast
urge	engender	cipher	pierce
emerge	stitch	plunder	wreak
wager	collide	determine	overrule
rumble	discard	recline	cast
commit	pretend	slide	blend

3. Calculate the following:

2^2
4^4
3^2
5^2
4^3
6^3
3^4

4. The Pythagorean Theorem is used to find the hypotenuse of a right triangle. The hypotenuse is the long side of a right triangle, which is opposite the right angle. The Pythagorean Theorem is stated as:

$$c^2 = a^2 + b^2$$

In the formula, *a* and *b* represent the two short sides and *c* represents the hypotenuse. To solve, square the two short sides and add them together. You would then need to find the square root of the results. When doing this on a spreadsheet, it is sometimes easier to break the formula down into two parts. For example, in one cell would be the sum of the squares of the two sides. In the next cell could be the square root of the results. If you wish, you can put the entire operation in one cell or you might wish to break it down into two steps.

Find the hypotenuse of the following right triangles:

Side a	Side b
3	4
20	15
16	12
12	9
18	24

Save the file as **SS1-21**.

Objectives

In this section, you will practice the following word processing skills:

- Set tabs, including decimal tabs
- Create indents
- Format text for boldface and underline
- Enter and edit text
- Print and save documents

In this section, you will build the following academic skills:

- Recognize appropriate spelling, capitalization, punctuation, and sentence construction within the context of a written passage
- Evaluate appropriate word and sentence choice
- Read for understanding
- Generate a written comparative composition
- Demonstrate an understanding of measurement concepts using metric and customary units

Activity 3-1

EXPRESSIVE VERBS

Enter the expressive verbs listed as shown. Set tabs to have four columns. Center and boldface the title at the top of the document. Save the document as **WP3-01**.

Activity 1-22

PROPORTION

When working with proportion problems, it is very important to set up the problem correctly. Proportion problems involve three numbers, two of which are related to each other.

An example of a proportion problem is:

Jerry has noticed that two ribbons on his printer will print 420 pages. How many pages can he expect to print with three ribbons?

In this example there are two ribbons for 420 pages, so these two numbers are related. The problem is to determine how many pages three ribbons will print. Mathematically, we would say the 2 is related to the 420 as the 3 is related to what? Or:

$$\frac{2}{420} = \frac{3}{x}$$

First you would multiply the 3 times the 420 and the 2 times the x. To solve, you would then divide the product of 3 times 420 by the 2. On a spreadsheet it can be done with one of the formulas as shown below. Note that when using some software, a formula must be preceded by a plus (+) and other software requires formulas be preceded with an equal sign (=).

	A	B	C	D
1	Ribbons	Pages	Ribbons	Pages
2	2	420	3	+(C2*B2)/A2
3				
4	2	420	3	=(C4*B4)/A4

The ratio or proportion should always be set up the same. For example:

$\frac{\text{Ribbons}}{\text{Pages}} = \frac{\text{Ribbons}}{\text{Pages}}$ and would *never* be $\frac{\text{Ribbons}}{\text{Pages}} = \frac{\text{Pages}}{\text{Ribbons}}$

Unit

OneTwoThree

123

You can save the following problems in the same spreadsheet file.

1. Armado Mendoza is an engineer for the television cable company. He is in charge of building bases for television antennas. It takes 260 pounds of gravel to make 4 cubic feet of concrete. How much gravel does Mr. Mendoza need to make the following cubic feet of concrete: 9, 11, 16, 21, 25?

	A	B	C	D
1	Gravel	Concrete	Concrete	Gravel
2	260	4	9	
3	260	4	11	
4	260	4	16	
5	260	4	21	
6	260	4	25	

2. Alex works for the Ballard Lawn Service. It is his job to spray a fungicide on customers' yards. Two gallons of fungicide will cover 400 square feet. How much mixed fungicide will he need for the following areas?

 1,200 sq. ft.
 2,400 sq. ft.
 8,000 sq. ft.
 9,000 sq. ft.
 12,000 sq. ft.
 15,000 sq. ft.

3. Misty is reading a blueprint of a house. The drawing is on a quarter-inch scale. A quarter inch equals one foot. Determine the number of feet represented by the following lengths:

 2 inches
 3 inches
 1 inch
 4 inches
 0.5 inches
 2.5 inches

Activity 2-19

Open the database **DB1-14**. Delete the field showing the building in which the teacher is located. Delete the records for Rick McDaniel and Chalna Trawick.

Teacher Name	Degree	Subject	Building	Students
Janice Early	MS	Math	C	120
Shawna Tankersley	BS	Math	C	130
Susan Ellis	BS	Math	C	100
Katie Craddock	MS	Eng	A	140
Chalna Trawick	MS	Eng	A	130
Gwen Green	BS	Eng	A	145
Carolyn Schofield	MS	Sci	D	140
Rick McDaniel	BS	Sci	D	100

Save the revised file as **DB2-19**.

4. Luci Liang is in food preparation for the Golden Formosa Restaurant. An eight-serving recipe calls for 1 3/4 cups of uncooked rice. How many cups of uncooked rice are needed for the following servings? Format the answers to two decimal places.

   12
   16
   20
   24
   28

5. If it takes Mandy two hours to enter 15 pages, how many pages can she enter in the following amounts of time? Format the answers to two decimal places.

   6 hours
   12 hours
   5.5 hours
   18 hours
   3.25 hours

6. Plan a party for all the computer students in your school. Take a survey of your class to determine how much each student would eat and drink. Find out how many people can be served by a one-liter soft drink. Also determine how many people a large pizza, a large package of chips, and a dozen brownies will serve. Find out how many computer students are in your school.

   Once you have taken your survey, calculate how many pizzas, liters of soft drinks, large packages of chips, and brownies will be needed for all the computer students in the school.

Save the file as **SS1-22**. Close the file.

Activity 2-18

Add the following fields to your database of homes, **DB1-13**. Save the revised file as **DB2-18**.

Address	Interest Rate	Years
1409 Holley	10	30
418 Ellis	9.75	20
1226 Powers	8.75	30
78 King Blvd.	8.75	15
1920 Jester	9	30
555 Travis	8	15
19 W. Coy	10.25	30
8080 Python	9	30

Activity 1-23

FRACTIONS

Start your spreadsheet software and open file **T123**. If you are not using the template disk, open a new spreadsheet. In either case, continue with the following instructions.

In this activity you will solve problems involving fractions. When you enter a fraction in a cell on a spreadsheet, the fraction will be converted to a decimal. On some spreadsheets an equal sign must be entered before entering the fraction.

For example, the fraction $\frac{1}{4}$ would be entered as =1/4.

On other spreadsheets, just enter 1/4. When the fraction is entered, it will be printed in the cell in decimal form (.25).

The spreadsheet will perform the mathematical calculations, but you will need to know which numbers are added, multiplied, divided, or subtracted. In this activity, you will be determining the fractional part of a whole. For example, a typical problem might be: There are 120 students in a room; 1/4 of them are seniors. How many seniors are in the room?

The first step is to state the problem. For example:

What is 1/4 of 120?

Translate the statement into a formula using mathematical symbols:

Word	Mathematical Symbol
What	x
is	=
of	*

The problem might be written: x = 1/4 * 120. To solve the problem on a spreadsheet, multiply the cell containing the 1/4 by the cell containing the 120.

Group 4

Country	Male Life Exp	Female Life Exp
Argentina	67	74
Nicaragua	61	66
Panama	73	77
Paraguay	71	74
Venezuela	71	78
Brazil	62	68
United States	72	79
Jamaica	72	76
Haiti	53	55
Cuba	74	79
Honduras	64	68
Colombia	69	74

For example:

	A	B	C
1	Fraction	Students	Seniors
2	.25	120	+a2*b2

or

	A	B	C
1	Fraction	Students	Seniors
2	.25	120	=a2*b2

You can save the following problems in the same spreadsheet file.

1. Jo Anne is setting up a monthly budget for the money she earns from her part-time job. She earns $280 per month. Her budget is shown below.

   1/5 for savings
   1/8 for clothing
   1/4 for entertainment
   1/10 for charity
   1/8 for transportaion
   3/20 for food
   1/20 for gifts

   Set up a spreadsheet to calculate how much money she has to spend for each item in her budget. Enter each fraction in such a way that it will be converted to a decimal with three decimal places. Format your answers to two decimal places with a dollar sign. Your spreadsheet may appear as shown below.

	A	B	C	D
1	Budget Item	Fraction	Earnings	Amount
2	Savings	0.200	280.00	
3	Clothing	0.125	280.00	
4	Entertainment	0.250	280.00	
5	Charity	0.100	280.00	
6	Transportation	0.125	280.00	
7	Food	0.150	280.00	
8	Gifts	0.050	280.00	

Group 2

Country	Male Life Exp	Female Life Exp
Uganda	50	52
Gambia	47	51
Algeria	66	68
Zimbabwe	60	64
Ghana	53	56
Liberia	54	59
South Africa	62	67
Mozambique	46	49
Zaire	52	56
Egypt	58	62
Ethiopia	50	53
Chad	39	41

Group 3

Country	Male Life Exp	Female Life Exp
Cambodia	48	51
Indonesia	59	64
Iran	64	66
India	57	58
Vietnam	63	67
Philippines	62	68
North Korea	66	72
Laos	48	52
Myanmar	57	61
Bangladesh	55	54
South Korea	67	73
Singapore	73	78

2. Of the 12,000 seats in the high school stadium, 1/6 are reserved seats. Of these reserved seats, 1/20 are for the pep squad, 1/25 are reserved for the flag corps, 1/40 are reserved for the drill team, and 3/50 are reserved for the band. The remainder of the reserved seats are reserved for the season ticket holders. How many seats are used by each school organization and how many seats are available for the ticket holders? Format your answer with commas.

3. At a recent motorcycle show, there were seven motorcycle manufacturers represented. Shown below are the number and makes of the motorcycles. Determine what percentage of the participants each manufacturer represents. Format your answer for percent with two decimal places.

36 Hondas
30 Kawasakis
24 Yamahas
20 Suzukis
15 Moto Guzzis
45 Harley-Davidsons
10 Huskys

4. Megan went to a sale at a store. She bought the following items on sale:

Item	Original Cost	Discount
Shoes	129.00	1/4
Dress	90.20	1/2
Pants	55.30	1/8
Blouse	28.30	1/6
Ring	134.60	1/3

The discount is the amount off the original cost. You may first have to determine the discount.

How much did Megan pay for each item, and what was her total cost? Format the answers with two decimal places.

Objectives

In this section, you will practice the following database skills:

- Add fields to a database
- Delete records from a database
- Delete fields from a database

In this section, you will build the following academic skills:

- Work with geographical data
- Work with consumer education data

Activity 2-17

Add the following fields and data to your database on countries, **DB1-12**. *Exp* is an abbreviation for *Expectancy*. Save the revised database as **DB2-17** and a 1, 2, 3, or 4 to indicate on which group you are working (e.g., **DB2-171**).

Group 1

Country	Male Life Exp	Female Life Exp
Belarus	66	76
Georgia	67	73
Tajikistan	64	70
Slovakia	69	77
Ukraine	65	75
Latvia	64	75
Slovenia	70	78
Macedonia	70	76
Russia	63	74
Azerbaijan	65	73
Croatia	67	74
Moldova	64	71

5. Assume the administrator at your school is considering building a new computer room. It has been decided to move computers from each existing computer room into the new computer room.

   It has been decided to move 1/8 of the computers in your room to the new computer room. How many computers would be moved?

   If 1/8 of the male students in your room were moved to the new computer room, how many male students would go to the new room? If 1/8 of the female students in your room were moved to the new computer room, how many female students would move?

Save the file as **SS1-23**. Close the file.

	A	B	C	D	E	F	G	H
1		Code	Bod. Injur.	Prop. Dam.	UM	PIP	Collision	Total
2	Augsburg	16	75	72	40	42		
3	Sukai	13						
4	Hawk	10						
5	Shark	12						
6	Kaito	8						
7	Lourve	14						

2. How much does it cost to own a car? Set up a spreadsheet and enter the following information in the first and second columns.

Augsburg	$35,000
Sukari	$27,000
Hawk	$21,000
Shark	$15,000
Kaito	$14,500
Lourve	$19,800

In the third column, enter the annual interest rate of the car loan as 11%. In the fourth column, enter the term of the note as 48 months. In the fifth column, calculate the payment.

Skip two rows and make six new columns. In the first new column, enter the names of the cars. In the second column, calculate the total cost of the auto loan. In the third column, calculate the insurance you would pay over the term of the note (four years). Remember that the insurance costs you have calculated are for six months. In the fourth column, enter the value of the car after four years. Get the value of the car from Activity 2-15. Place the cost of the car for four years in the fifth column. The cost of the car for four years is the total amount you have paid, plus the insurance, minus the value of the car after four years. In the sixth column, calculate the average cost per year over the four years.

Save your work as **SS2-16**.

Activity 1-24

GEOMETRIC FORMULAS

You have a room that needs carpet. It is necessary to find the number of square feet and square yards to determine how much carpet you will need. A student wants to paint her room. She has to determine the surface area of the walls to find out how much paint to buy. David is putting a new roof on his house. How many squares of shingles will he need to buy?

All the above situations require use of a geometric formula to find the solution. The types of problem found in this activity are the types of problems that people deal with every day. Fortunately, geometric formulas do not use complicated math.

You may wish to refer to the formulas in the table when you are working the geometric problems. Remember that spreadsheet software does not "assume" multiplication. Therefore, the calculation to determine perimeter, 2 (l + w), would be entered on the spreadsheet as 2 * (l + w).

In the formulas, *s* is side, *l* is length, *w* is width, *r* is radius, *b* is base, and *h* is height. Use 3.14 for pi (π).

Perimeter	square rectangle	$P=4s$ $P=2(l+w)$
Circumference	circle	$C=2\pi r$
Area	square rectangle triangle trapezoid circle	$A=s^2$ $A=lw$ $A=\frac{bh}{2}$ $A=\frac{1}{2}h(b_1+b_2)$ $A=\pi r^2$
Surface	cube cylinder (lateral)	$S=6s^2$ $S=2\pi rh$
Volume	rectangular prism cylinder cube	$V=lwh$ $V=\pi r^2h$ $V=s^3$
Pythagorean Theorem	right triangle	$c^2=a^2+b^2$

Activity 2-16

PAYING FOR YOUR RIDE

Start your spreadsheet software and open file **T216**. If you are not using the template disk, open a new spreadsheet. In either case, continue with the following instructions.

You can save the following problems in the same spreadsheet file.

1. Insurance companies establish their rates based on several factors. These factors are the age and driving record of the driver, the county and state where the car is insured, and the type of car.

   Automobile insurance consists of several parts. Part of the insurance premium is to provide insurance to other parties in case they are hurt or to pay for property damage. Part of the premium is to pay for damage to the insured's car. This is called collision. The more the car will cost to repair or replace, the higher the collision part of the insurance.

   Cars are given rating codes. These codes are used to determine the amount of collision insurance. Place the Car Code and the Amount of collision insurance for each code on the spreadsheet.

Car Code	Amount
8	197
9	205
10	249
11	261
12	295
13	317
14	350
15	385
16	454

The bodily injury, property damage, UM (uninsured motorist), and PIP (personal injury protection) are the same for all the cars. These rates are based on the driver and the county and state in which the car is driven. The collision is based on the insurance code for the car. The amounts are for six months of insurance. Try using the LOOKUP or VLOOKUP feature of the spreadsheet to place the correct collision amounts in the Collision column. Total the figures in each row.

You can save the following problems in the same spreadsheet file.

1. Debbie Hunter's apartment has the following room sizes measured in feet:

	A	B	C	D
1	Room	Length	Width	Area
2	Living Room	16	14	
3	Dining Room	12	12	
4	Kitchen	12	10	
5	Bedroom	14	12	
6	Bathroom	10	8	
7			Total	

a. Calculate the square feet of each room.

b. What is the total square feet of the apartment?

2. Calculate the area of the following circles (round to the nearest hundredth):

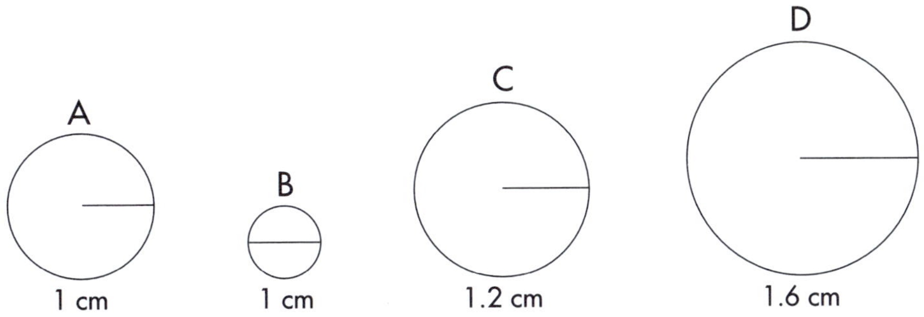

3. Darren is placing a roof on a shed that is 23 feet by 52 feet.

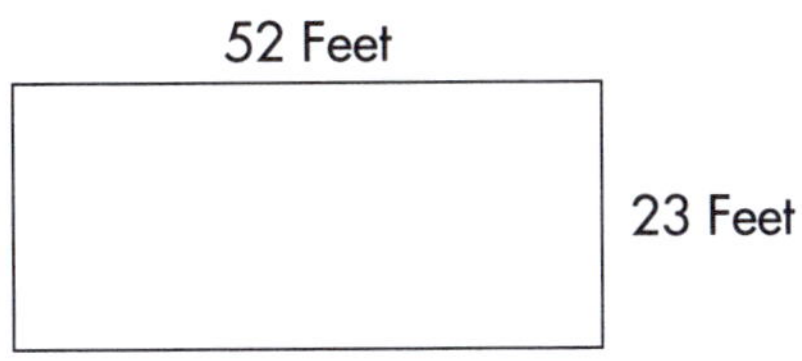

2. Depreciation is the loss in value of a car. Following are six cars, their prices, and their depreciation factors.

Car	Price	Depreciation Factor
Augsburg	$35,000	0.07
Sukari	$27,000	0.08
Hawk	$21,000	0.11
Shark	$15,000	0.10
Kaito	$14,500	0.08
Lourve	$19,800	0.09

The formula for calculating depreciation is:

Current Value = P- (P x (YR + 1) x DF)

In the formula, *P* is the original price of the car, *DF* is the depreciation factor, and *YR* is the age of the car. Set up a spreadsheet that will calculate the value of each car when its age is one, two, three, and four years old.

	Value 1	Value 2	Value 3	Value 4
Augsburg				
Sukari				
Hawk				
Shark				
Kaito				
Lourve				

Enter the formula to calculate the value of each car when it is one, two, three, and four years old.

Save your work as **SS2-15**.

a. How many square feet is the roof?

b. Shingles are sold by the square. A square is 100 square feet. If shingles cost $43 a square, how much will it cost to shingle the roof?

4. Jason has four pastures that need to be fenced. He is planning to use a four-strand barbed-wire fence for each. Find how many feet of barbed wire he will need to fence the following pastures, which are measured in feet. Format your answers with commas.

Length	Width
210	210
300	210
450	300
450	210

5. How much would it cost to paint your classroom? First you will need to find the area of each wall in the room. If a gallon of paint will cover 200 square feet of surface area, how many gallons of paint will be required to paint the room? If the paint costs $16 a gallon, how much will it cost to purchase the paint? The members of your class will volunteer to apply the paint, so there will be no cost for labor. Also assume that brushes and cleanup supplies are provided by class members.

Save the file as **SS1-24**. Close the file.

Activity 2-15

You can save the following problems in the same spreadsheet file.

1. Which is a better deal, a cash rebate or lower interest? Determine the total cost of the following cars. Your columns should be as follows:

Car	Price	Rebate	Int. Rate	Mos.	Payment	Total Cost

Dealer A
- Car: Augsburg
- Price: $35,000 minus $3,000 rebate ($3,000 off price of car)
- Interest Rate: 12%
- Monthly Payments: 48

Dealer B
- Car: Augsburg
- Price: $35,000
- Interest Rate: 4%
- Monthly Payments: 48

Dealer C
- Car: Hawk
- Price $21,000 minus $3,000 rebate
- Interest Rate: 10%
- Monthly Payments: 60

Dealer D
- Car: Hawk
- Price: $21,000
- Interest Rate: 5%
- Monthly Payments: 60

Dealer E
- Car: Kaito
- Price: $14,500 minus $2,500 rebate
- Interest Rate: 11%
- Monthly Payments: 36

Dealer F
- Car: Kaito
- Price: $14,500
- Interest Rate: 4%
- Monthly Payments: 36

Activity 1-25

AMERICAN STANDARD CODE FOR INFORMATION INTERCHANGE (ASCII)

Computers are number machines. They only deal with numbers. When you enter a letter of the alphabet from the keyboard, the computer changes the letter to a number. Each letter of the alphabet and each symbol on the keyboard is represented by a code. In fact, other symbols that are used in documents, but which are not on the keyboard, are represented by a code. An example of a symbol not on the keyboard would be the pi symbol, .

This code is called ASCII. ASCII stands for the American Standard Code for Information Interchange. For example, the capital letter *A* is assigned the number 65. A lowercase *a* is assigned the number 97. A capital *B* is 66 and a lowercase *b* is 98. When you press an uppercase *A* on the keyboard, the computer converts that to the number 65 and the screen displays an uppercase *A*. The computer performs this calculation very quickly. How quickly can you convert ASCII codes to the letters they represent?

The letters are numbered consecutively. From the information given, see if you can decode the following:

65	83	67	73	73			
67	79	77	80	85	84	69	82
75	101	121	98	111	97	114	100

Enter the codes (numbers) and your answers in a word processing document. Save the file as **WP1-25**.

Write a message to another student in ASCII to decode. Have the other person write you a message and decode their message.

When trying to solve this problem with your spreadsheet, do not change the payment. Enter the down payment, interest rate and term of the note (four years) and change the principal (price) until the payment gets within one dollar of $250. Include sales tax. What would be the total cost of the car? How much would you be paying in finance charges (cost of the loan)?

4. What is the highest priced car you could afford if your car payment could be no greater than $350 per month based on:

   a. Down payment of $2,500?

   b. Interest rate of 16%?

   c. Five-year loan?

   The price of the car should be to the nearest $100. Include sales tax. What would be the total cost of the car? How much would you be paying in finance charges?

Save your work as **SS2-14**.

Activity 1-26

THE HUNT FOR RAM VIRUS

Overview

A team of computer hackers has been terrorizing the state. These hackers have gone from town to town and placed a virus on the local computer club's bulletin board. They are known as the RAM Virus Gang. Your team has been assigned the task of tracking down a member of the RAM Virus Gang.

The good news is you will have some help. A former member of the gang will give you clues so that you can track down the gang member. The bad news is this person is a former computer math teacher. This person takes perverse delight in giving clues in strange ways. The clues are given as math problems, some even as word problems. Your team will need to apply the necessary math skills to solve the clues.

The good news is that you will be given a map. The bad news is that after the clues are given out, you cannot use the map. You will need to design a database in which to place the information from the map. There will be a clue telling you at which town to start. The following clues will send you from town to town. After each clue is solved, you will know how far and/or which direction to go to the next town (e.g., travel 14 miles or go to the northwest). You must design a database in such a way as to be able to follow the clues to track down the RAM Virus Gang.

Once you find the town, how do you know how to find the gang member? Easy—members of the RAM Virus Gang always stay in an RV park in a red and violet trailer. Your job is just to find the town. The local authorities can do the rest.

Setting Up the Database

You will need to use the map given to you by your teacher. Design a database that can be used to follow the clues to track down a member of the RAM Virus Gang. The first clue will tell in which town to start. Each clue after the first clue will give you a direction to travel and/or the number of miles to travel. You will not have a map at which to look. You will need to use your database to follow the clues. There may be more than one way to design the database. You may wish to divide the map, with each team member responsible for one section of the map.

Activity 2-14

DID YOU GET A GOOD DEAL?

Select a computer program to calculate the payments and the total cost of buying a car. The total cost of buying the car is calculated by multiplying the monthly payment by the number of payments. The sales tax is calculated on the price of the car. You may set up your document as follows:

Price	$14,500.00	Sales Tax	8%
Down Payment	$5,000.00	Months Financed	48
Amt. after Down Pay.	$9,500.00	Interest Rate	11%
Sales Tax	$1,160.00		
Amount Financed	$10,660.00		
Payment	$275.51		
Total Cost	$18,224.64		

Calculate the following with an 8% sales tax. Format dollar figures as currency (dollar signs, commas, and two decimal places). You can save the following problems in the same spreadsheet file.

1. What would be the payment of a $12,000 car with a $2,000 down payment at 15% interest for four years?

2. What would be the payment on a $25,000 car with a $5,000 down payment at 14% for five years?

3. What is the highest priced car you could afford (to the nearest $100) if your car payment could be no greater than $250 per month based on:

   a. Down payment of $3,000?

   b. Interest rate of 15.25%?

   c. Four-year loan?

The map is not exact. Not all directions are due east, west, north, and south. For some mileages given, it may be unclear if the miles are to the next town or to the next crossroads. You will have to use your best judgment as to what to enter in your database.

Save the database as **SS1-26**. Close the file.

6. Lending institutions often include the home insurance payment as part of the monthly house payment. These institutions insist that the house be insured and the payments be kept up-to-date in case the house is destroyed.

    The base insurance premium on Mary and Gary's house is $575.00 for six months. Because the premium is going to be paid monthly, there is an added charge of 12%. What is the monthly amount of the insurance on the house?

7. Mary and Gary selected Greater Barnard State Bank for their loan. What will be their monthly house payment with the property tax and insurance included?

Save your work as **SS2-13**.

Activity 1-27

THE HUNT FOR RAM VIRUS

The Tracker Sheet

Your teacher will tell you which member of the RAM Virus Gang you will be tracking. You will need to solve the math problem to know where to begin. The clue will tell you the city where you will begin your search. At the end of each clue will be a math problem to solve in order to know the number of the next clue. Each clue will tell you which direction to travel and/or the number of miles you must travel. Of course, since the clues are given by a former computer math teacher, you must solve a math problem in order to understand the clue. Create a Tracker Sheet to chart your progress.

On your Tracker Sheet, enter in the row for Clue 1 the number of the first clue and the town where you begin. On each following line enter the number of the clue, the direction and/or number of miles, and the name of the town reached. You may not reach a town on every clue. You will have reached the town where the gang member is hiding when you reach the last clue. You can tell it is the last clue because there will not be a math problem leading you to any other clues.

P.S. Don't forget to look in the red and violet trailer in the RV park.

Create a Tracker Sheet like the one shown below. Save the document as **SS1-27**.

Tracker Sheet

Clue	Clue Number	Town	Direction	Miles
1				
2				
3				
4				
5				
6				
7				
8				
9				

2. Use the MIN and MAX functions to find the lowest and highest Total Cost of Loan.

3. Notice that in certain cases it is possible for the total cost of a much more expensive house to be only slightly more than the total cost of a less expensive house. On a $100,000 house, how much total cost could you save between a 15-year loan and 30-year loan at the same interest rate? Enter the answer on the spreadsheet under Question 2.

4. Mary and Gary are buying a house. The amount of money they will need to borrow to purchase the house is $100,000. Some places at which they have applied for a loan are going to charge points. Points are a fee to get a loan and are expressed as a percentage of the loan. For example, four points would be a charge of 4% of the loan. The lending institutions also charge closing cost. This is a charge for surveys and other work required to process the loan. The points charged and closing cost are paid in advance and are not part of the money borrowed. Mary and Gary are trying to determine from which lending institution to borrow the money. Find the monthly payments and total cost of the house for each one of the following:

   Suburban Tulia Savings and Loan: Interest rate is 10.25% for a 25-year loan. They charge 3 points, and the closing cost is $860.

   Greater Cumby Metro Savings and Loan: Interest rate is 10 3/8% for a 30-year loan. There are no points, and the closing cost is $900.

   First Noonday Federal: Interest rate is 9 3/4% for a 30-year loan. They charge 3.5 points and the closing cost is $500.

   Greater Barnard State Bank: Interest rate is 10% for a 25-year loan. They charge 2 points, and the closing cost is $750.

5. When you are making a house payment, you often are paying more than just your mortgage payment. Your house payment often includes the taxes on the property and your home insurance. The tax is based on the assessed value of a piece of property. The assessed value is a percentage of the true market value of property. The property tax is a percentage of the assessed value.

   Assume that the market value of Mary and Gary's house is $100,000. The assessed value is 80% of the market value. The tax rate is .0033 of the assessed value. If the property tax is divided by 12 and paid each month, what would be the monthly payment?

The Clues

For Map A

Horace "the keyboard" Johnson	Start at clue 1/4 of 240
Bruce "the mouse" Duncan	Start at clue 4.25% of 400

For Map B

Eddie "monochrome" Milham	Start at clue 9 1/2% of 1,800
Judy "the sound blaster" Grantham	Start at clue 34% of 500

[2] Thirty-two is to 128 as what number is to 312? This is the ASCII code for the direction you travel. Next clue: number of inches in two feet.

[3] The ASCII code for the direction you travel is seven dozen minus one. Next clue: 9 squared.

[6] What percent of 680 is 469.2? This is the ASCII code for the direction you travel. Next clue: number of inches in a yard.

[8] Find 40% of 195. Find 1/16 of 1,104. The previous two numbers are the ASCII codes for what two letters? Put the letters together to determine which direction to travel. Next clue: number of minutes in 1 3/4 hours.

[12] Eight is to 40 as what is to 45? The answer is the number of miles you travel. Next clue: number of ounces in a gallon.

[13] Travel the same direction you would go if you were traveling from Washington state to Florida. A building has 468 square feet. One side is 18 feet long. The other side is the same as the number of miles you should travel. Next clue: 7 squared.

[15] Travel the same direction you would go if you were traveling from Texas to Maine. A foundation for a building has 3,250 square feet. One side is 325 feet long. How long is the other side? Travel that number of miles. Next clue: 18 squared.

[17] This town has two words in its name. The first word is associated with petroleum products. The second word means a place where people live. Next clue: 16.5% of 1,800.

Activity 2-13

THE PLEASURES OF HOME OWNERSHIP

How much do you think you end up paying for a $100,000 house if you have a 30-year loan at 10 3/4%? Buying a house is the largest single purchase most people make. It is important to know the cost involved in home ownership and how to make wise decisions when financing a home. Making a wise decision when getting a home loan (called a mortgage) can save you as much as the home costs.

In this activity, you will need to use the payment function of the spreadsheet you are using. The payment function requires you to enter the cell address of the principal (the amount you are borrowing), the interest, and the number of payments. Since house payments are normally paid monthly, you will need to calculate the length of the loan in months and enter the interest rate per month. This is determined by taking the yearly interest rate and dividing it by 12. In this activity, format the Cost of House with dollar signs. Format all other the dollar figures with commas and two decimal places.

You can save the following problems in the same spreadsheet file.

1. Determine the monthly payments, the total cost of the house, and the total costs of the following home loans. Calculate the Number of Months by multiplying Number of Years by 12. The Total Cost of House is determined by multiplying the number of payments by the amount of the monthly payment. The Total Cost of Loan is the difference between the amount you pay back, which is the same as the Total Cost of House, and what you borrow (Cost of House).

Cost of House	Interest Rate	Number of Years	Number of Months	Monthly Payments	Total Cost of House	Total Cost of Loan
$50,000	10.5%	15				
$50,000	10.5%	30				
$50,000	9.0%	15				
$100,000	10.5%	15				
$100,000	10.5%	30				
$100,000	9.0%	15				
$60,000	9.0%	15				
$60,000	10.5%	15				
$60,000	10.5%	30				

[19] Five numbers total 302. Four of the numbers are 20, 22, 80, and 102. The fifth number is the ASCII code of the direction you travel. Next clue: 14 squared.

[20] Travel 19.308 kilometers. Next clue: 5/8 of 160.

[21] Take 1/4 of 348. The answer is the ASCII code for the direction you travel. Go to 12.75% of 1,600.

[24] Find 12 1/2 percent of 80. That is the number of miles you travel. Next clue: square root of 225.

[26] Take the median of the following numbers: 5, 47 102, 90, and 83. Find the mode of the following numbers: 69, 100, 120, 69, and 103. This two numbers represent the ASCII code of the direction you travel. Next clue: 16 squared.

[32] Go 32.18 kilometers. Next clue: 1/8 of 48.

[36] The number of miles you travel is 3/15 of 105. Next clue: number of feet in a yard.

[49] The average of five numbers is 26. Four of the numbers are 64, 10, 22, and 16. Find the town that is the same number of miles away as the missing number. That is your final destination.

[52] What is 1/8 of 120? Travel that number of miles. Next clue: square root of 361.

[60] This town has the same name as a president of the United States. His nickname was "Old Hickory." It is the name of the largest town in Mississippi. Next clue: 1 1/4% of 1,680.

[72] Find the square root of 144. Travel that number of miles. Next clue: number of ounces in a cup.

[81] Forty is to 140 as the miles you travel is to 28. Next clue: square root of 676.

[100] Start at twelve noon. Add the following times: 1 hour 40 minutes, 2 hours 45 minutes, 1 hour 15 minutes and 1 hour 50 minutes. The direction the hour hand is pointing is the direction you travel. Next clue: 4/5 of 420.

15,000	8.00%	60
25,000	7.50%	60
100,000	9.75%	300
50,000	8.75%	180

2. When you borrow money, you pay back more than you borrow. To determine the total amount you pay back, you can multiply the monthly payments by the number of payments. This is sometimes called Total Payments. Calculate the total amounts you pay back for the preceding loans. Format the total amounts you pay back as currency (dollar sign, commas, and two decimal places).

3. The interest you pay on a loan is the cost of borrowing the money. Basically, you are renting money. It is important to know how much it costs to borrow money, which is sometimes referred to as the cost of the loan or the finance charge. The cost of the loan is determined by subtracting the amount borrowed (the principal) from the total amount you pay back. Calculate the costs of the loans with which you have been working. Format the costs of the loans as currency (dollar sign, commas, and two decimal places).

Place your name on the spreadsheet and save the file as **SS2-12**. Print the spreadsheet.

[105] Twenty-one is to 140 as what number is to 80? Travel that number of miles. Next clue: square root of 169.

[121] Travel in the same direction you would if you were going from Oklahoma to Oregon. Next clue: 3/4 of 200.

[128] Add these times: 45 minutes, 30 minutes, 1 hour 20 minutes, and 1 hour 25 minutes. Travel the direction the hour hand would be pointing if you added these times to midnight. Next clue: number of weeks in a year.

[150] A room has one side that is 13 feet and has a perimeter of 44 feet. The length of the other side is the amount of miles you will need to travel. Next clue: 7/14 of 380.

[170] The town at which you start is between Reveille and Aaron. Perhaps it was named after a southern Civil War general that helped Lee at the battle of Antietam. Next clue: 87.5% of 600.

[171] You will leave a town that has the same name as the name of the football bowl game that is played on January 1, in Dallas, Texas. It is also the name of the leading crop raised in the south before the Civil War. Next clue: 22% of 550.

[190] What is 12.5% of 624? This number is the ASCII code of what letter? What percent of 200 is 138? This number is the ASCII code of what letter? Put the letters together to determine the direction to travel. Next clue: number of inches in a foot.

[196] A room has 210 square feet. One side is 14 feet. The other side is the number of miles you travel.

[204] The next town is 25.75 kilometers away. Next clue: 7/10 of 400.

[280] Start at noon. Add these times: 2 hours 30 minutes, 3 hours 45 minutes, 2 hours 15 minutes, and 2 hours 30 minutes. Travel in the same direction the hour hand would be pointing. Next clue: 8/9 of 81.

[256] A driver takes 40 minutes to go 20 miles. It took this driver 30 minutes to reach your destination.

Objectives

In this section, you will practice the following spreadsheet skills:
- Format numbers in a spreadsheet and output for a spreadsheet
- Use the payment function
- Enter formulas
- Use a lookup table

In this section, you will build the following academic skills:
- Evaluate variables, expressions, and formulas
- Solve equations involving integers and decimals
- Analyze or solve problems

Activity 2-12

Start your spreadsheet software and open file **T212**. If you are not using the template disk, open a new spreadsheet. In either case, continue with the following instructions.

Most spreadsheet software has the ability to calculate payments. In order to calculate payments, you must have the amount borrowed (principal), the interest rate of the loan (sometimes referred to just as rate), and the number of payments. The number of payments is sometimes referred to as the term of the note. If the payments are made monthly, as in the case of most home and car loans, the interest must be entered monthly. To determine monthly interest, you divide yearly interest by 12.

1. Calculate the monthly payments on the following loans. The first figure is the loan amount, the next is the yearly interest rate, and the last number is the number of monthly payments. Use the payment function of the spreadsheet. Since you are making monthly payments, you will need to divide the yearly interest by 12 to determine the monthly interest rate. Check the software manual for exact details on the payment function for the spreadsheet you are using. Format the payments as currency (dollar sign, commas, and two decimal places).

[297] Calculate 1/8 of 552. This is the ASCII code for the direction you travel. Next clue: 1/6 of 120.

[324] The average of five numbers is 34. Four of the numbers are 56, 48, 20, and 12. Find the town that is the same number of miles away as the missing number. That is your final destination.

[336] Find the square root of 49. That is the number of miles you travel. Next clue: number of cups in a pint.

[525] Go in the same direction you would travel if you were going from Kansas to Nebraska. Next clue: 1/3 of 96.

I loved all those wonderful movies like Casablanca and Teenage Mutant Ninja Turtles on my cutesy little veezey (that's my pet name for it). It had a 30-day warranty, and the machine stopped working on the thirty-first day. That is just my rotten luck; I am the kind of person who parks the car and steps right in the mud puddle. Every time!!! Well, anyway, since the machine is still very new, I feel your warranty should cover the damage; don't you see. There was a film in it at the time, and the snooty video rental store has charged me $5 damage for it. I would also like to be reimbursed for that. I purchased the VCR at your store on March 13.

Please let me know whether you wish to repair or replace the machine. I will return it to your store. Thank you for your cooperation. Bye now!

Sincerely,

Unit

OneTwoThree

123

Activity 2-11

THE PERSUASIVE DOCUMENT

In this activity, you will need to rewrite a letter to persuade a business to repair a VCR that is no longer covered by warranty.

The first paragraph should state your position very clearly and should say what it is you want done. Briefly mention (introduce) the material that will be explained in the body. In the body, arrange the facts in chronological (time) order. The concluding paragraph should restate the main idea in words different from the introduction. A polite last sentence is appropriate. Delete all unnecessary remarks. Be sure there is no slang.

Check and correct punctuation and capitalization needed for the greeting (salutation) and closing. Be sure all sentences are complete (no run-on sentences or sentence fragments). Underline movie titles. Format the letter in block style. Enter your name under *Sincerely*. Save the document as **WP2-11** and print.

```
420 Tophill
Arp, Texas 75703-3019

(Today's Date)

Acme Furniture Company
456 Other Street
Anytown, Texas 77777-6451

Ladies and Gentlemen:

How are you? I am fine, thanks. The VCR I purchased from
your store n March has malfunctioned. Drat, phooey!  I
was just about to watch my favorite movie, Born Free,
about the lionesses, and I wanted to sit right down and
bawl in my popcorn over my bad luck!!! I would like you
to repair or replace the machine.
```

Objectives

In this section, you will practice the following word processing skills:

- Open new and existing word processing document
- Format text for alignment, underlining, and boldface
- Enter, typeover, insert, delete, and find and replace
- Print and save documents

In this section, you will build the following academic skills:

- Recognize appropriate spelling, capitalization, punctuation, and sentence construction within the context of a written passage
- Evaluate appropriate word and sentence choice
- Generate a written persuasive composition

Activity 2-1

ROBOTICS—I

Start your word processing software and open the file **T201**. If you are not using the template disk, open a new word processing document and enter the following document exactly as shown. Underline and boldface as shown. Center the title at the top of the document.

Robotics

One aspect of computer technology that most fascinates people is the robbot. Modern americans can envision the day when computer-controlled robots will take over the drudgery of tasks or go into very dangerous situations to work. In the medical profession, robots assist in surgery because they can work more precisely and their hands are smaller than human hands. The robotic hand can go into the brain, for example, in a far smaller hole and with much less damage to the patient than a human surgeon's

Organization Editor
Evaluation

Name: ______________________________________

Writer's Name: ______________________________________

Date: ______________________

Class Period: ________________

Your paper shows good organization because you:

A way the organization could be improved would be to:

The first paragraph is good because:

A way to improve the first paragraph would be to:

The best reason given in the composition is:

One of your reasons could be improved by stating it in this way:

The best example or explanation of a reason is:

An example or explanation that could be improved is:

The best elaboration is:

A way to improve one of your elaborations would be to:

The closing paragraph is good because:

A way to improve the closing paragraph would be to:

drilling and cutting. **The robot could go in to drain abscesses, to implant radioactive pellets into cancers. Or to guide laser beams to do surgery or repair damage.** The patient needs less anesthesia and recovers (6) when less cutting is involved. The surgical robot is accurate to within two one-thousandths of an inch. A robotic technician must be intelligent, careful, and (7). **<u>The future for robotic technology is bright, an exciting opportunity for a person who is intelligent and who is willing to work.</u>**

Save the document as **WP2-01**. Close the file.

ORGANIZATION EDITOR

As the Organization Editor, you will look at the overall organization and effectiveness of the persuasive composition. Is it well-organized and do you think that it will effectively persuade the audience to which it is targeted? The paper needs to be authoritative, but should not insult or offend the audience.

The papers must be properly organized. The first paragraph must start with a strong sentence that is not stated as an opinion. The sentence should leave no doubt about the writer's position on the issue addressed. The first paragraph includes the arguments or reasons that the writer intends to develop in the composition. The paragraph should end in a transitional sentence that leads to the second paragraph.

Each paragraph in the body of the composition is used to elaborate one of the reasons that the writer has used in the opening paragraph. The paragraph should contain specific examples that support the reason. It is important that rich and vivid verbs, adjectives, and adverbs, as well as figurative language, are used to make a strong impression on the reader. Examples, quotations, and comparisons are good forms of elaboration. The last sentence is a transitional sentence leading to the next paragraph.

The ending paragraph is an overall summary of the composition. The paragraph summarizes each of the reasons for the writer's position. The paragraph also tells the audience the action the writer wants taken.

Check the sentence structure in the paragraphs. Is there a variety of sentence structure, or are all the sentences the same type and the same length? Make sure there are no run-on sentences or sentence fragments. Be sure to complete all of the evaluation form.

Activity 2-2

ROBOTICS—II

Open the document called **WP2-01**. Make the following corrections. Save the document as **WP2-02**.

1. In the underlined parts, correct any error in spelling.

2. In the underlined parts, correct any error in capitalization.

3. In the underlined parts, correct any error in punctuation.

4. In the boldfaced part that is not underlined, select one of the following choices to correct any run-on sentence or sentence fragment. Leave the passage as it is if no correction is needed.

   a. The robot could go in to drain abscesses, to implant radioactive pellets into cancers, or to guide laser beams. To do surgery or repair damage.

   b. The robot could go in to drain abscesses, to implant radioactive pellets into cancers. Or to guide laser beams to do surgery to repair damage.

   c. The robot could go in to drain abscesses, to implant radioactive pellets into cancers, or to guide laser beams to do surgery or repair damage.

5. Select from one of the following choices the best way to improve the underlined, and boldfaced part. Leave the passage as it is if no correction is needed.

   a. The future for robotic technology is bright. Robotic technology is an exciting opportunity for a person who is intelligent. A robotic technician must also be willing to learn. He must also be willing to work.

   b. The future for robotic technology is bright, an exciting opportunity for a person who is intelligent. And willing to learn and work.

   c. The future for robotic technology is bright. This future is an exciting opportunity for a person who is intelligent and willing to learn and work.

ELABORATION EDITOR

The job of the Elaboration Editor is to make sure the paper uses effective elaboration to support powerful arguments. The elaboration can be in the form of quotations, examples, explanations or comparisons. Using a full and varied vocabulary is a way of providing powerful elaboration.

Check the papers of the team members to make sure each paper contains active verbs, powerful adjectives, and colorful adverbs. The use of effective adverbs and adjectives paints a more vivid picture for the reader. Encourage the writers to use active verbs rather than passive verbs. For example, "The cat was in the bushes" is not as interesting as "The cat patiently lurked in the bushes."

Figurative language can make the examples more effective. Use similes, metaphors, personification, and hyperboles to win the reader to the writer's point of view. Examples that are well-elaborated are more convincing than examples without elaboration.

Work with each member of the team to provide more powerful elaboration for the examples. On a blank piece of paper, draw a chart similar to the one following. Work together to fill in the chart with as many descriptive words and as much figurative language as possible. Refer to the list of expressive verbs and power words used in Activity 1-10.

Reason	Examples Explanations	Descriptive Words

Under the descriptive words, list adjectives, adverbs, and figurative language that you might use to elaborate each example.

6. Replace the (6) with the best choice from the words listed below.

a. faster
b. more fastly
c. rapider
d. more fast

7. Replace the (7) with one of the choices listed below.

a. goodly trained
b. trained good
c. well-trained
d. good trained

Work with the writer to develop a chart that will show the plan for the paper. A chart might appear as:

Position

Reason 1 (Arguments) Examples	**Reason 2 (Arguments) Examples**	**Reason 3 (Arguments) Examples**
1.	1.	1.
2.	2.	2.
3.	3.	3.
4.	4.	4.

Activity 2-3

WORD PROCESSOR—I

Enter the following paragraph exactly as shown.

WORD PROCESSOR

Many experienced typists have resisted learning how to use the computer or word processor because they think that it is too complex, that it is too difficult to learn, or that it will slow them down. None of the arguements is valid. The word processor is a marvelous invention, and a good typist who wants to can master it in a few days. The computer is faster more accurate and easier to use than a typewriter when making corrections. **The typist who already knows the keyboard can learn a few function keys. Practice to become familiar with the new device, and then be fairly fast and accurate in a short period of time.** If the program has a spelling check device, many of the errors will be pointed out for correction. **Do not, however, rely too heavily on the machine. It will not find all the errors**. Corrections are as simple as scrolling to the error, backspacing, and reentering. Paper can be saved by correcting on the screen before printing. Editing can be done by block-moving segments of text. Most people who ____ to use word processors would never choose to go back to the typewriter as ____ primary office tool.

Place your name flush right at the top of the document.

Save the document as **WP2-03**. Close the file.

ARGUMENTS EDITOR

As the Arguments Editor, it is your responsibility to make sure that the paper of each member of your team develops strong and effective reasons for the position being taken on the issue. Part of your job will be to make sure all members of the team work together to select good reasons for the position the writer of the paper is taking.

First, have everyone on the team take out a blank piece of paper. The team members should write their positions or opinions at the tops of their papers. Taking one paper at a time, the team should come up with as many reasons as possible to support the position stated in the first sentence. All the reasons should be written down by the writer of the paper. Use brainstorming to list all the reasons you as a team can think of to support the writer's position. In brainstorming, it is important not to criticize the reasons given but just to come up with as many reasons as possible. When the team has exhausted all the reasons for one position, you should move on to another member of the group and brainstorm reasons for that person's opinion.

After this has been completed for all members of the team, you will need to work individually with each team member. Go over the list with each team member. Examine each reason or argument on the list. Make sure the argument makes sense, is appropriate for the audience, and is directly related to the topic. Draw a single line through each reason or argument that you and the writer feel is not a good reason. A reason is not appropriate if your audience thinks it will not benefit anyone, is not necessary, is not important to society, does not relate to personal values, or the cost is not reasonable. Work with the writer to select three to five of the strongest reasons. It is important that all reasons stay on the topic.

Each reason is to be supported by specific examples. To be effective, the examples must not be opinions but facts. The examples must be specific and relate directly to the reason. The reasons must also appeal to the audience.

Activity 2-4

WORD PROCESSOR—II

Open the document **WP2-03**. Make the following corrections. If no error exists, leave the passage as it is.

1. In the underlined parts, correct any error in spelling.

2. In the underlined parts, correct any error in capitalization.

3. In the underlined parts, correct any error in punctuation.

4. In the boldfaced part that is not underlined, select one of the following choices to correct any run-on sentence or sentence fragment. Leave the passage as it is if no correction is needed.

   a. The typist who already knows the keyboard can learn a few function keys, practice to become familiar with the new device, and then be fairly fast and accurate in a short period of time.

   b. The typist who already knows the keyboard can learn a few function keys practice to become familiar with the new device and then be fairly fast and accurate in a short period of time.

   c. The typist who already knows the keyboard can learn a few function keys, practice to become familiar with the new device. And then be fairly fast and accurate in a short period of time.

5. In the underlined and boldfaced part, select one of the following choices to correct any run-on sentence or sentence fragment. Leave the passage as it is if no correction is needed.

   a. Do not, however rely too heavily. On the machine. It will not find all the errors.

   b. Do not rely too heavily on the machine, however, because the machine will not find all the errors.

   c. Do not rely too heavily on the machine because the word processor will not find all the errors, however.

Step 4

Revise your paper and use the ideas from the team that you think are good. After you have revised the paper, have the members of the team proofread the document. This can either be done on the computer screen or using a hard copy of the document. All members of the team need to check the papers for any spelling, punctuation, or capitalization errors. Check the papers for subject-verb agreement, proper verb tense and form, and correct case of pronouns.

Place your name, date, and class period centered at the top of the document. The names of your team members should be centered at the bottom of the document. Print and save the document as **WP2-10**.

6. Select the best word or words from the following to place in the first blank.

   a. learns
   b. learn
   c. learning
   d. will have been learning

7. Select the best word from the following to place in the second blank.

   a. his
   b. her
   c. their
   d. its

Save the document as **WP2-04**.

Activity 2-10

THE PERSUASIVE COMPOSITION—II

You will write a persuasive composition of three to seven paragraphs. The opening sentence is important and you will need to use the same techniques for this multiparagraph composition that you used in Activity 2-9. It is important to make use of effective verbs, adjectives, and adverbs. Remember, you are trying to persuade the reader to believe your opinion is the correct one. Very importantly don't forget your audience. Who you are addressing will affect both your wording and your reasons.

Step 1

Write a persuasive composition of three to seven paragraphs. You should take a position either for or against one of the following:

Students should not be allowed to wear shorts to school.

Handguns should not be sold in the United States.

Animals should not be used for experimentation.

After the paper is completed, save the document as **WP2-101**.

Step 2

Incorporate the suggestions from the teacher lecture into your paper. Save the revised document as **WP2-102** and print a copy of the document for each member of the team (including yourself).

Step 3

Work with other members of your team to make improvements to your paper. Each team member will have a responsibility to complete an evaluation form and make specific suggestions for improvement on each paper. Next, as a team go over each paper and discuss the improvements that are needed. It is important that each paper in the team be as well-written as possible. Each paper should be unique in that it reflects the ideas and opinion of an individual, not the team.

Activity 2-5

COPYRIGHT LAW—I

Start your word processing software and open the file **T205**. If you are not using the template disk, open a new word processing document and enter the following paragraph exactly as shown. You will have an opportunity to correct the mistakes later.

```
    The Copyright Law of the united states guarantees the
right of authors to publish, use, and perform their
"Writings." Other people cannot copy a published work and
claim it. Wrongfully claiming what someone else has
written is called plagiarism. To claim the copyright, the
arthur simply puts a notice in the front of the book
before it is sold to the public. The copyright law also
covers plays movies art music, videotapes, and computer
programs. An author can register unpublished work with
the U.S. Copyright Office before it is ready for sale to
the public. If the author wants that protection.
```

Underline the following:

> "The Copyright Law of the united states guarantees the right"
>
> "is called plagiarism. To claim the copyright, the arthur"
>
> "The copyright law also covers plays movies art music, videotapes, and computer programs."

Boldface the following:

> "An author can register unpublished work with the U.S. Copyright Office before it is ready for sale to the public. If the author wants that protection."

In the underlined parts, correct any errors in spelling.

In the underlined parts, correct any errors in capitalization.

Step 4

Make the needed corrections to your document on the word processor. After you have made the corrections, make sure other members of the team proofread your paragraph. You will need to check the paragraphs of the other team members as well.

Center the names of the team members under the paragraph. There should be four blank lines between the paragraph and the names.

Print the paragraph and save the document as **WP2-09**.

In the underlined parts, correct any errors in punctuation.

In the boldfaced part, replace the sentences with one of the following choices if a correction is needed. If no correction is needed, leave the sentences as they are.

a. An author can register unpublished work with the U.S. Copyright Office before it is ready for sale to the public if the author wants that protection.

b. An author can register unpublished work. With the U.S. Copyright Office before it is ready for sale to the public if the author wants that protection.

c. An author can register unpublished work with the U.S. Copyright Office. Before it is ready for sale to the public. If the author wants that protection.

Save the document as **WP2-05.**

Activity 2-9

THE PERSUASIVE COMPOSITION—I

In a persuasive composition, you are trying to convince someone of some thing. You will take one side of an issue and attempt to persuade the reader to be either for or against the issue. In persuasive writing, you will incorporate many of the skills of descriptive writing and also use techniques suited particularly for persuasive writing.

Step 1

Write a five-sentence paragraph either for or against one of the following:

> MTV should not be part of standard television service, but should be available for an extra charge.
>
> Pep rallies should only be before or after school and not during school hours.
>
> We should not send our surplus grain to other countries without getting something in return.

At the top of the document, center your name, the date, and the class period. Skip two lines between the class period and the paragraph. The paragraph should be double-spaced.

Save the document as **WP2-091**.

Step 2

Apply the suggestions made by the teacher. After the document has been modified, double-space and print the corrected document. Be sure the revised document is saved as **WP2-092**.

Step 3

Work with other members of your team to make improvements in the paragraphs written by your team members. Work together and evaluate each paper as a team. All persons in the group should make suggestions for the improvement of the paper.

Activity 2-6

COPYRIGHT LAW—II

Open the document **WP2-05**. Key the following two paragraphs a double-space below the last paragraph. Enter the document exactly as shown.

```
   The exclusive right of an author lasts 28 years, and
the author may apply for renewal for another 28 years.
Copyright protection in foreign countries also exists as
long as a country has an exchange agreement with the
United States. The author generally has the protection of
that (6) laws. Most countries (7) a copyright period of
50 years or the author's lifetime plus 50 years.

   Anyone may read, watch, listen to, or enjoy a
copyrighted work. No one can, however, make copies of it,
sell it, or publish it as that person's own. That is the
right of the creator of the work.
```

Boldface and underline the following:

> "Copyright protection in foreign countries also exists as long as a country has an exchange agreement with the United States."

Replace the underlined and boldfaced sentence with one of the following choices. If no correction is needed, leave the passage as it is.

a. Copyright protection in foreign countries also exists. As long as a country has an exchange agreement with the United States, protection exists.

b. Copyright protection in foreign countries also exists. It exists as long as a country has an exchange agreement with the United States.

c. Copyright protection in foreign countries also exists. It exists under certain conditions. These conditions are that that country has an exchange agreement with the United States.

Activity 2-8

RIGHT TO PRIVACY—II

Open the document **WP2-07**, and add the following paragraph exactly as shown.

```
   Today's computers have made it possible for snoops to
know nearly everything about almost everyone, and (A) is
no way to protect against it. Banks, credit card
companies, mailing list handlers, retailers, and
governments all think (B) need to know and share all
kinds of information about citizens. When the spread of
information started, many people did not object because
they thought (C) might help catch crooks and control
fraud. Now many people think it has gone too far. (D)
want the easy exchange of information to stop. They do
not want (E) tax business, banking business, buying
habits, and telephone calls to be available to any
computer hacker. Many Americans think (F) we are entitled
to another right like the ones guaranteed in our Bill of
Rights, and that is the right to privacy.
```

Use search and replace to replace the letters in parentheses with one of the following words. Some of the words may be used more than once.

1. their
2. there
3. that
4. they
5. it

When complete, save the document as **WP2-08**.

Replace the (6) with one of the following choices:

a. countries'
b. countries
c. countrys'
d. country's

Replace the (7) with one of the following choices:

a. have
b. has
c. had
d. are

Save the document as **WP2-06**.

Activity 2-7

RIGHT TO PRIVACY—I

Start your word processing software and open the file **T207**. If you are not using the template disk, open a new word processing document and enter the following document exactly as shown. Add a double-space between lines.

```
   Tw& h>ndr*d y*@rs @g& &>r c&nst#t>t#&n wr#t*rs fr@m*d
th* B#ll &f R#ghts, wh#ch #s d*s#gn*d t& pr&t*ct th*
c#t#z*ns. Th&s* wr#t*rs m*@nt t& g>@r@nt** &>r p*rs&n@l
r#ghts @nd fr**d&ms. F&r m@ny y*@rs, @m*r#c@ns *nj&y*d
th* r#ght t& pr#v@cy. @s l&ng @s @ p*rs&n d#d n&t
#nt*rf*r* w#th &th*rs, @n @m*r#c@n c&>ld l#v* @ n&rm@l,
pr#v@te l#fe. Th@t #s n& l&ng*r p&ss#bl*. Th* fr@m*rs &f
th* B#ll &f R#ghts c&>ld n&t p&ss#bly h@v* f&r*s**n th*
c&mp>t*rs &f th* tw*nt#*th c*nt>ry. #f th*y h@d b**n @bl*
t&, th*y m#ght h@v* *n@ct*d @n *l*v*nth #t*m #n th* B#ll
&f R#ghts t& m&r* *xpl#c#tly g>@r@nt** &>r fr**d&m &f
pr#v@cy.
```

After the document is entered, use find and replace to replace the symbols with the correct letters. Each symbol represents a specific letter of the alphabet. For example, all the @'s might represent the letter j (but they don't).

After the document has been corrected, save the document as **WP2-07**.

Appendix C

Database Basics

WHAT IS A DATABASE?

A database allows small or large amounts of data to be organized and accessed more efficiently. Automated databases are electronic filing systems that store and retrieve data. A good example of a database is a traditional file cabinet that contains folders. File cabinets is one method of organizing data. Here are three of the many benefits to using an electronic filing system.

1. Information is retrieved quickly and easily.
2. Records and information can be managed easily.
3. Information can be stored usefully.

Database software looks very similar to a spreadsheet. They both have columns and rows, a formula bar where information is entered, and so on. Spreadsheets are primarily used for analyzing data. However, database software is used to store and retrieve data. Databases are usually much larger than spreadsheets. Databases are much larger because they are used for long-term storage of information.

PARTS OF A DATABASE

Like other applications software, the database screen for a Windows program has a title bar, menu bar, scroll bar, status line, and toolbar. The database screen also includes a formula bar, like spreadsheet software. There are several different features of database software that you should be familiar with—fields, data, field name, entry, record, and record name.

IBM OR COMPATIBLE SYSTEMS

DOS programs are generally stored on a hard disk. If you are using a computer that has a hard disk drive or is connected to a network, DOS will load as you turn on the computer. DOS is the system that Microsoft Windows runs on top of. Rather than learn all of the DOS instructions for operating an application, you can simply point to an icon (pictorial representation) and Windows will run the program. This software uses icons to represent programs and groups related programs in a window. What is so wonderful about all programs designed to run on Windows' GUI (graphic user interface) is they have similar features such as files are opened, saved, and printed in the same way; commands are often the same from program to program; even screens look the same from program to program. After learning one Windows program, it is very easy to learn another program.

Starting Windows

You will need to follow these steps to load Windows:

1. Turn on your computer. The computer will go through the loading process. When this is finished, your screen will probably show the hard disk prompt, **C:**.
2. At this point your computer may automatically load Windows and show a screen call Program Manager. If it does not, key **WIN** at the **C:>** prompt and press ENTER.

Using a Mouse

It is important that you learn to use a mouse before using a Windows-based program. The mouse moves the pointer around the screen. Begin by placing your hand over the mouse and moving the mouse until you see the pointer on your screen. Now move it left or right. If you move the mouse off of the mouse pad, pick it up and bring it back onto the pad. Here are some important terms that you should be familiar with:

- *Pointer*—An arrow that moves around the screen as the mouse is moved.
- *Single click*—Press down once on the left mouse button.
- *Double click*—Press down twice consecutively on the left mouse button; an hourglass appears on the screen. The hourglass lets you know to wait until a process has been completed.

- *Click and drag*—Press and hold down the left mouse button while moving the mouse.

- *Select*—Point to an icon and single click on the left mouse button.

If you need to, review these Windows terms before starting any of the applications software:

- *Title bar*—The top line in any open window that contains the program name and/or the filename.

- *Control button*—A symbol on the left side of the title bar that looks like a minus sign. By moving the mouse pointer to the Control button and double clicking, the window closes and becomes an icon at the bottom of the screen.

- *Maximize button*—An up arrow on the right side of the title bar. A single click on the Maximize button will enlarge that window to fill the entire screen.

- *Restore button*—A double-headed arrow that replaces the Maximize button when a window is maximized. A single click on a Restore button changes the window to its former size.

- *Minimize button*—A down arrow on the right side of the title bar. A single click on the Minimize button reduces the window to an icon at the bottom of the screen.

- *Group icons*—Icons at the bottom of the Program Manager screen. These icons represent groups of related software programs. You can open a group by double clicking on a group icon.

File Information

Assigning Filenames and Extensions

All data files must be assigned a filename. A filename consists of one to eight characters. Try to have your filename reflect the data stored in that file. Filenames can be made more specific by using an optional extension. A filename extension consists of a period followed by one to three characters. Some programs will automatically assign an extension if you do not do so.

Copying Files
You will use this command often to make working copies of program and data disks. Another use for COPY is to make a backup copy of a disk to avoid loss of data. The copy command can be used to copy individual files or an entire disk.

Erasing/Deleting Files
From time to time, you should remove unneeded files from your disk. The ERASE command or DEL (delete) command will erase or remove a file from a disk. Be careful when using this command because once a file has been erased, it cannot be easily recovered.

Working with Directories

When you need to view a file on your disk, the computer will not search the entire disk for the file. Rather, the file directory is searched. This directory, which is created when the disk is formatted, is called the root directory. To better organize your files, you can create multiple levels with subdirectories. The root directory is the highest level directory of a disk.

Creating Subdirectories
You can create a subdirectory to group all files of a similar type together. It is easier to locate files that are organized by related groups than to search randomly through all the files on a disk.

Changing Directories
You can key **CD** and the subdirectory name and press ENTER to move from one subdirectory to another.

MACINTOSH USERS

For the Macintosh to function, you need to have two types of software. The first software is the system that operates the computer and enables it to display and manage the files. Second, the Finder software is also essential in operating the Macintosh. When the computer is first turned on, the first program to run will be Finder, which shows the Desktop. The Finder/Desktop empowers you to easily work with and manage your files and diskettes.

Starting the Macintosh

If you are working with a hard drive, you can start the system by turning it on. If you are working with two drives, first insert the system disk in one of the drives before turning on the computer. If you are working with a network system, you must first insert the start-up disk.

When the Finder/Desktop is displayed, an icon on the screen will identify whether you are using a hard disk, a floppy disk, or a network to start you computer.

Initializing a Disk

If you want to store files on a new disk, the disk must first be initialized. This is done by following these steps:

1. Insert a new disk in the drive. If necessary, eject the system or startup disk by dragging the Disk icon to the Trash icon, then release it. You will need to use either a new disk or a disk that contains data that can be erased. Note: Initializing erases all files stored on the disk.
2. Click on either the One-sided or Two-sided box to indicate whether you are Initializing a single-side or double-side diskette.
3. Click on the Erase box.

Naming the Disk

Once the disk has been initialized, name the disk by keying up to 27 characters (do not use a colon), then click on OK. When the disk has been initialized and named, an icon showing the name of the disk will appear on the desktop.

Naming Files

You must assign a filename to all data files. A filename must consist of 1 to 31 characters and cannot contain colons. The filename should reflect the data stored on it.

Creating Folders

In an office, documents are stored in folders in a cabinet. Macintosh uses this same concept to organize files. To create a folder, choose the File New Folder command or press COMMAND + N.

Copying Files to Another Folder

Files can be copied from one folder to another folder by dragging the file to the new folder. A dialog box appears, showing a scale that indicates how much has been copied during the copying processing.

Removing/Deleting Files

Delete files by dragging the file to the Trash icon. The end of the pointer must be within the Trash icon when the mouse button is released. When this is done correctly, the Trash icon should be displayed in reverse.

Removing/Deleting Folders

Folders can be removed by dragging them to the Trash icon. The end of the pointer must be within the Trash icon when the mouse button is released. When this is done correctly, the Trash icon should be displayed in reverse.

Emptying the Trash

As you delete files and folders, the Trash icon will become enlarged. If you decide not to delete a file or folder before you empty the Trash, you can drag the file out of the Trash can. To discard the files you deleted, you must empty the Trash.

Appendix B

Spreadsheet Basics

WHAT IS A SPREADSHEET?

A spreadsheet is a tool that allows users to analyze numerical problems. It is organized into columns and rows, and data are entered into the intersections of the columns and rows. The column and row intersections are known as cells. With an electronic spreadsheet, formulas or calculations rules may be entered in addition to text and numbers. When you enter a formula in the electronic cells, the program calculates the results instantly. When a formula that affects another cell is entered, the contents of the affected cell also change automatically.

Most electronic spreadsheet programs operate in the same way. A cursor is used to identify the cell in which data are to be entered. The programs perform various commands using special command keystrokes or menu selections, and they save and retrieve the spreadsheet to and from a disk file.

BEGINNING SPREADSHEET GUIDELINES

You will need to prepare your own data disk on which you will save the exercises you enter or modify. All exercises will be saved to a directory or folder. All spreadsheet exercises may be completely entered using keystrokes. If you are using a template disk, you may load most exercises and follow the instructions to complete them.

Check for errors before saving or printing. If a formula is needed, you may use any formula that produces the correct calculation.

- *Fields*—A category of information contained in a database.
- *Data*—The specific information within a field is known as the data. Data could consist of an identification number, first name, and last name.
- *Field name*—A label that usually appears at the top of a database column which describes the kind of information that will be stored in the column.
- *Entry*—Each piece of information that is keyed into a field is called an entry.
- *Record*—All of the information about one person would be considered a record.
- *Record name*—Each record has a record number that is shown at the left side of the screen.

Appendix A

Operating Systems Information

OPERATING SYSTEM SOFTWARE

It would not be possible to use your computer without the computer's operating software. This system provides the computer with the ability to communicate with applications or integrated software packages. Some different types of operating systems are MS-DOS, OS/2, and Windows 3.1 for IBM and compatible computers. Macintosh computers use an operating system such as System 6 or System 7.

APPLICATIONS AND INTEGRATED SOFTWARE PACKAGES

You are probably familiar with at least one type of computer software. That software is a word processing program. A word processing program is an example of an applications software package. An applications software program allows you to do task like creating documents, calculating tables, sorting data, and creating pictures and illustrations. Some applications programs that you might be familiar with are Lotus 1-2-3 for Windows for developing spreadsheets and dBASE IV for managing databases.

Academic Applications with Technology introduces you to application and integrated software. This type of software combines four popular computer applications: word processing, database management, spreadsheet analysis, and communications. Integrated software can be used for applications such as preparing a business letter (word processing), making a list of geographical information, and recording income and expenses (spreadsheet). Documents and information can be exchanged quickly from one application to the other.

MOVING AROUND THE WORKSHEET

The horizontal rows of a spreadsheet are numbered consecutively on the left side. The columns are identified by letters. The column letters start at the letter A and go through the letter Z. They also run from AA to ZZ, BA to BZ, and so on.

The black outlined area is known as the selector or cell pointer. The selector indicates the active cell in which data can be entered. The selector can be moved using the arrow keys or the cursor pad, or the mouse. Some spreadsheet programs have a special function key that will automatically allow you to move between large areas on the worksheet.

ENTERING DATA

Spreadsheet data can be classified under two different types—labels and values.

- *Labels*—These are usually words or phrases composed of alphabetic characters. This type of data is usually used for explanatory labels for rows or columns. Numbers which are not used for calculation can also be used as labels. For example telephone numbers, identification numbers, inventory numbers, addresses, or ZIP code numbers are considered labels.

- *Values*—Values generally consist of numbers, @Functions, and special symbols that are used for calculations.